The People's Histo

Ashington Coal Company
The Five Collieries

Ashington, Woodhorn, Linton, Ellington, Lynemouth

by

Mike Kirkup

The Ashington Coal Company inherited Longhirst Colliery Village and its clarty backstreets. Here Cooper's van delivers oil to Mrs Lockhart in Straker Terrace, *circa* 1930s.

First published in 2000 by

The People's History Ltd
Suite 1
Byron House
Seaham Grange Business Park
Seaham
Co. Durham
SR7 0PY

ISBN 1 902527 62 3

Contents

These Woodhorn Colliery lads smashed the European record using a plough.
Back: 'Buck' Jones, Micky Chesterson, Mallan Stevens, John Cole, Ron
Patterson, Davey Davis, Bill Wake. Lad kneeling is Brian Ions.

Acknowledgements

The bulk of the research for this book was contained in the *Ashington Colliery Magazines*, dated 1921-40. Articles were also obtained from the *Ashington Advertiser* and the *Post*. Bruce Mather loaned a book on Instructions to Pit Trainees. Thanks are also due to others who have delved into local history such as Ross Miles, Bill Harrison and local journalist, Alan Robson. Photos have been loaned from many people, including Ron Staines, Ron Patterson, Bob Blacklock, Jim Nichol, Jean Stacey, David Brown, Brian Auld, Margaret Brannigan and many others. A special thanks to Bill Harris of Newbiggin, for making available his thoughts and pictures of the Miners' Strike of 1984-85. In conclusion, I am indebted to those folks who took photographs of long ago, never realising that one day they would form the basis of a history book; men such as Jack Wallace, Bill Harrison, Reuben Daglish, Jim Brooks, Brian Wade and Mike Parker.

Front cover: Dennis Waterman posing at Woodhorn in 1982 for his film 'The Captain's Tale.'

Back cover: Picket line at Ashington Central Workshops during the Miners' Strike in 1984. (Photo by Linda Stevenson.)

Introduction

Whether they planned it or not, the town of Ashington, and the villages of Linton, Lynemouth, Woodhorn and Ellington, was the creation of the Darlington-based Priestman family and their like-minded Quaker followers. And whatever their intentions, the lives of these mining communities were shaped and coloured by *their* early decisions and philosophy.

The Priestman family owned the Consett Iron Works and also became involved in running a coal mine at Rowlands Gill. The two industries prospered side by side. The Quaker influence manifested itself in the interest shown in their workers, both socially and spiritually. Jonathan Priestman was drawn to the Ashington area in the early 1860s after acquiring a substantial amount of shares in the Ashington project when his father died. He immediately bought more shares until he held a commanding position on the board of directors.

The valuable seam of coal, revealed when the Bothal Downcast shaft was sunk in 1867, also brought in William Milburn who became a principal shareholder in the first coal company, known as 'Milburn, Priestman & Partners'. The Milburns were a highly successful, wealthy family with control of most of the north-east shipping lines. Large swathes of land to the east of what is now known as Milburn Road all became part of the Milburn Estate.

From the outset, Priestman sought to bring in fellow Quakers as part of his management team. Mr H. Richardson, Robert Booth, Edmund O. Southern, J.J. Hall and Fred Booth, captained the team that laid down the solid, nononsense foundations from which the five collieries grew to such a huge and immensely profitable undertaking. There was reward for the resolute disciples, but swift punishment for anyone who trod a path other than that furrowed by the 'maisters'.

J.J. Hall

Fred Booth

And yet, with all their professed convictions of fair dealing, the Ashington Coal Company (renamed in 1898) was blatantly concerned in fostering their own image as humane, charitable owners, dedicated to the well being of their workers. But hidden away from the public view was the unacceptable face of capitalism: the pursuit of profit at the expense of long-term security for its workforce. In my opinion, it is they – the Ashington Coal Company – who are to blame for the premature demise of these five collieries.

Right from the first day it was palpably obvious that the company were after 'easy pickings'. The owners pinpointed the most commercially profitable seams and proceeded to run them dry. Coal of inferior quality, such as the seams of Middle Main, Bottom Main, Top Yard and Maudlin, were ignored until it was far too late. Some might argue that, as entrepreneurs, the ACC were in business to make money quickly for their shareholders, and that the company's only guilt lay in hypocrisy. Others, including miners' union leaders like Will Lawther and Joe Gormley, in books they wrote later, were less inclined to be so lenient with the early private coal-mining regimes of Britain.

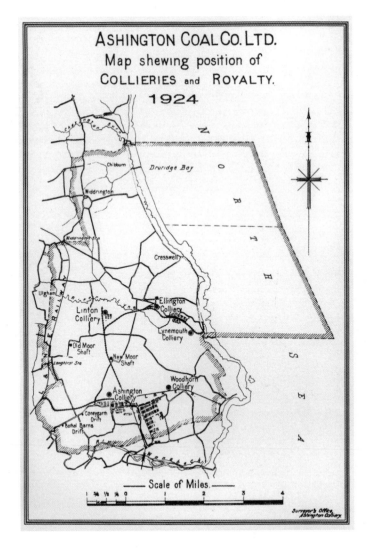

ASHINGTON 'A MODERN PIT VILLAGE', 1884

That was how it was described in the *Newcastle Chronicle* of January 1st 1884. The reporter went on to say: 'Ashington is in every respect a modern pit village, for it is only within the past twenty years that its once deserted plain has become a scene of busy life. The fields that produced the golden wheat and bearded barley now resound with the sound of industry, the tread of men, the cheery tones of female voices, and the merry prattle of children. When you scan the long rows of houses with their beautiful gardens, stretching over the village; view the fine triangle of schools at the further end; see the Methodist chapels, the stores, the Mechanics' Institute, the reading rooms and other institutions, it is almost impossible to conceive that they have all sprung up within so short a space.'

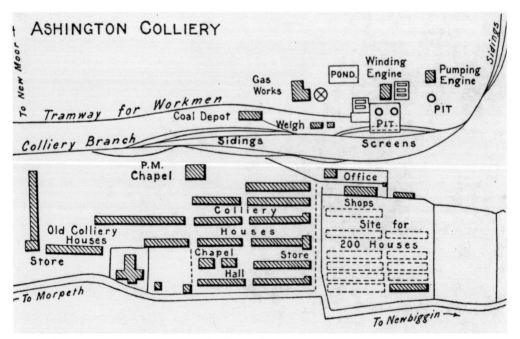

The photo on the previous page shows Ashington Colliery from the air in the 1920s when there were still six chimneys. This diagram is the layout of what the complex looked like in the 1880s. It shows a site left for '200 houses'. In fact, the 'top end' of Ashington eventually had over 800 miners' dwellings with its colliery rows from 1st to 11th, plus Long Row, Cross Row, Stable Row, New Moor and the Six Houses.

This is an artist's impression of what the first colliery looked like soon after it was erected. The same newspaper went on to say: 'Ashington is the latest of the Northumbrian pit villages, and it seems a model of what such a village should be. There was no stint of money when the houses were erected, a supply of excellent water is provided (from the pit itself) for the people, and by continual flushing of drains and constant supervision of outhouses (toilets), sanitary excellence is obtained. The everyday life of the Ashingtonians is enhanced by their educational facilities and social enjoyments. They possess a capital brass band which lately spent seventy pounds on new instruments.'

Five shafts were sunk at Ashington in the space of twenty years: Carl Upcast and Downcast in 1873; Bothal relief shaft in 1877; Duke Downcast 1885; and the Bothal Downcast in 1890.

Two shafts were sunk to the Grey Seam, depth 17 fathoms, and three others to the Low Main seam, depth 95 fathoms. (A fathom is six feet.) The Grey Seam was a particularly rich one at over six feet high in places. Other heights were Low Main 5ft 8ins; High Main 4ft 9ins; and Yard Seam 2ft 10ins. Only the upper part of the Grey Seam was worked and it included 1ft 3ins of coal and splint, most of which was brought to bank (surface).

Capital investment was later heaped upon the development of new pits at Woodhorn in 1894 and Linton in 1896. Ashington and district was no longer a baby with a hungry mouth. The region had grown into a healthy robust adolescent, looking for somewhere to spread its wings.

The Duke Pit sinkers were housed near what became Ashington Canteen, in a set of six houses, called … The Six Houses. Some of the sinkers on this photo are: Atchison, Martin, Purvis, Carr, Tours, Bell, Milburn, Turnbull, Alder and J. and A. Harrison.

Such was the importance of music to miners, the Duke Pit had its very own brass band, playing at many functions in the town. The band was initiated by the Hardy family. Front seated two boys: Joe Hudson and Thomas Hardy. First row: George White, Bill Byers, Bill

Maxwell, Thomas Hardy conductor, Bill Cole and Ed Robinson. Second front row: William Myers, unknown, Tom Myers, Bob Maxwell, James Lillico and James Hardy. Back row: Ralph Hardy, Phil Tait, W. Nuttall, Seppie White, Tom Fenwick, W. Tait, Jim Moore, Ken Johnson, Bill Robinson, R. Kelly, J.W. Baird, Jim Purdy, Tommy Temperley.

One of the first families to make their mark in Ashington were the Thompsons. George Thompson married Catherine Laws whose father Jack Laws helped to sink the first shaft. The Thompsons had eight sons and three daughters, and their first home was in the Sixth Row. Life underground was tough for George who started by hewing coal by hand; he eventually retired as a deputy, aged seventy-two. Outside the Thompson home, and all the others, was a board displaying the names of every working pitman in the house. Against each name was the time that man had to be called up for work. It was the job of the mother to make sure that no-one 'slept the caaller'. Photo shows Catherine and George in their sixties.

John H. Johnson (right) was not the first boy to be killed at Ashington Pit, nor was he the last, but his story is surely one of the most tragic. John was born at 83 Ninth Row, Ashington in 1897, attending the Bothal School, before leaving, aged fourteen, But his first day down the Bothal Pit was also his last. Like most young boys, he was assigned to a job near the shaft bottom, helping with the movement of coal tubs. John had only been there a matter of hours when a set of tubs got loose from the haulage rope – they were 'amain', to use the phrase of the experienced miner. They hurtled towards John, knocking him into the sump (bottom) of the shaft where he was immediately struck a fatal blow when crushed by the descending cage.

Joseph Martin was born in Allendale on November 5th 1853. He wrote:

'I was brought to Ashington – Fell 'em Doon as it was then – in the first week of February 1854. It was Mr Henderson and Mr Lee, the owners, who had persuaded my parents to come here. Then there were only seven houses in the Cross Row, and the Long Row was not completed. When old enough, I had to get up at seven o'clock every morning and go to Coney Garth Farm for the milk. The farm was kept by an old lady called Mrs Humphrey.

'I soon tired of going to school, and was only nine years of age when I applied to Mr Matthew Fayres for work at the pit. He started me on the Screens. There was no shelter of any sort then, and we stood picking stones in all weathers for eleven hours a day. For this work I was paid at the rate of a shilling a day.

'In the following year I went down the pit to look after a trap-door, after which I became a pony driver. A tiny pony named 'Duke', only nine hands high, often wandered down to the shaft bottom, and if he had half a chance he made off with somebody's bait.

'At that time the engine went night and day pumping water out of the pit, although we could not get any drinking water until the shift was over. Nobody worked about the pit at night except one brakesman who often had the doubtful company of tramps.'

Joseph Martin worked for the ACC for sixty-four years, retiring in 1928.

Right from the start, the miners were encouraged to form themselves into sporting teams. This is one of the earliest cricket teams seen at Ashington Rec in 1900. Back: W. Job, Stephen Ralph, Robert Laws, Nairn, James Sixsmith and T. Thompson. Centre: Conroy, unknown, unknown, Joseph

Waldock, Moses Sixsmith (a Woodhorn Road shopkeeper) and Thomas Hardy. Fred Beattie is seated centre; and reclining are Tom Atkinson, Joseph Morpeth and an unknown.

Records show that the game of cricket began in Ashington in 1865 at the place called Fell 'em Doon when Thomas A. Clarke got a few men together with a bat, ball and stumps, which he had made himself; they turned out on the ground on the north side of High Market. In those days, neither houses nor school had been built. The 'old' Rec was actually on a site later to house the Fifth Row.

A group of Ashington Blacksmiths taken in November 1905. Back row: E. Bell, W. Gillians, P. Shield. Second back row: T. Bland, Jack W. Lillico, J. Gillians, N. Chicken, J. McDonald. Third back row: J. Armstrong, R. Hall, W. Carr, F. Whinnom, T. Hogg, W. Jackson, C. Cook and N. Bell. Second front row: C. Wilken, J. Miller, J. Finlayson, J. Temple, J. Scott, T. Gownass. In front: E. Jackson, T. Lillico, D. Peary and J. Sinclair.

Ashington Cricket XI, 1904, made up mostly of colliery officials. Back row:
Andrew Eastwood umpire a retired miner, Dr Trotter, Mr Chambers former
head at North School, Mr Flint bank clerk, F. Croker Ashington pit deputy,
E.W. Milburn manager of Woodhorn Colliery, and Mr Greenwell a Co-op
butcher. Middle row: W.E. Pattison undertaker and joiner, Stanley Hickling
another North School headteacher, Jack Waldock, Jim Armstrong blacksmith,
and Peter Barrass an AUDC workmen. In front Joe Morpeth Ashington deputy,
and Ben Clavering who moved to Netherton.

Ashington Colliery in 1906, looking west, was a massive concern with the
pityard spread over many acres of ground. You can see how close the nearest
colliery houses were built on the left through the smoke of a burning brazier.

Badgered by Forster's 1872 Education Act, the ACC were forced to build an elementary school for their workmen's children. This became known as the Bothal School because of a link with a previous school of that name at Bothal Village. In the early 1900s, the head was Mr J. Gray, seen here in 1908 with the school's football team, most

of whom went on to work at the colliery. The team had been successful in winning the league, the Nursing Cup and the Henderson Cup as well. Back row: W. Lawrence, F. Freeman, W. Hart. Middle row: Mr Masterson and Mr H. Gray, W. Johnson, J. Abercrombie, Mr J. Gray, A.S. Crow, W. Purvis, Mr J. Pattison and Mr Wilson. Front row: W. Smith, R. Hope, Tom Cook, George Bowart and Jack Pattison.

This 1910 group of Ashington joiners includes back row: J. Andrews, R. Morton, G. Ruddick, W. Young and Harry Turnbull. Second back: ex-sergeant W. Lillico, W. Robinson, T. McConnel, Jack Fairfax, D. Morton, J. Davison, Walter Laseby and George Turnbull. Second front row: J. Scott, G. Brown, R. Murray, A. Pollard, T. Strong, J. Athey and Fred Farnell. Front row: T. Thornton, G. Gray, C. Sweet, E. Young and G. Young.

The first motor car ever to come into Ashington was a model T Ford. It was purchased by J.J. Hall and was a four-seater with a tourer body. Closed cars were not known in those days. Not even side screens had been invented. It was bought on February 6th 1912 and nearly seven years later it was transferred to the Ashington Coal Company. The two rear seats were removed and a small body made for it in the Joiners' Shop. And so it became 'The Ford Flat', a vehicle of some notoriety. It was probably one of the first self-advertising vehicles, and it was said you could see it

coming a mile away. Especially if the sun was looking at it, as it had brass rods with which to prop up the windscreen, brass lamps, and a brass radiator. It was looked after by a man we only know as 'Hughie'. We do know it once collapsed near the Miners' Theatre and had to be carried ignominiously back to the pit garage on a wheelbarrow. On another occasion it was set upon by two dogs in Station Road, a skirmish that saw the Ford subside on to the pavement with two broken wheels. Eventually, the front part of the vehicle became so dilapidated that a new one was built which completely enclosed the driver. This must have invigorated the old Ford so much that it went berserk one day and burst through a hedge at New Moor. It also had a one-to-one with butcher John Wheatley's premises where it ran amok. A quick wrench on the steering wheel by the driver only saw the hapless car career into a gate post and turn turtle. It only took two bystanders to haul it upright.

Young lads could leave school at thirteen in those days if they could prove they had a job to go to. And that job, inevitably, was down the pit after their father had put in a good word for them with the colliery overman. First job for a young boy was to work as a 'datal hand' on the underground haulage system which traversed the mine. Here we see a 1920s boy demonstrating how 'not' to hang a set of tubs on to the rope. He should be standing at the side of the track rather than in it. He is not using a cap-lamp and he is wearing a muffler (scarf), both of which would indicate that he was working at the shaft bottom where it was electrically lit and extremely cold.

Joe and Jonty Abercrombie were two well-known Ashingtonians. Joe was born in 1887, went to the Bothal Pit as a laddie, and he was still there when he died in 1954 at the age of sixty-seven. Said his daughter, Nellie, mother of opera singer Maureen Williams: 'One of the other onsetters at the Bothal Pit, Andra Hall, told me one day: "Nellie, yor father has worked like a trooper all his life and it's high time he retired." But he wouldn't.'

Jonty Abercrombie joined the Army and fought in the Boer War of 1900. He won the Military Medal in the 1914-18 war, and was later a fore-overman at Ashington Colliery, and Major in the Home Guard during the Second World War. Joe Abercrombie won many prizes for walking, training at the Rec for hours on end.

Seen here on the left in his walking gear with trophies and brother Jonty, his trainer, seated; the other two, also trainers, were Bob Wardhaugh and Jock Wardle.

This particular steam train was laid on specially in the 1960s for train buffs. It is seen here approaching Ashington Station, and you can see how far the mountains of pit waste stretched, even in the sixties. At night they often flared up and could be seen for miles around.

An Offices XI here, this time from 1912. Most of these men went on to senior positions with the Coal Company. Back row: Arthur Tait assistant cashier, John McCoy assistant cashier at Lynemouth, Tom Collins, Tom Ledgerwood who emigrated to Australia, Jim Henderson stores manager, Sid  Crowe secretary to the Agent, and John Coulson group cashier. Front row: Jack Graham who, like Tom Collins, was killed in the First World War, Bob Wade cashier at Woodhorn, Gregor Anderson, Dickie Howe who later ran the Welfare Department with Commander Kemp, and Fenwick Gibson who went on to manage a colliery in County Durham.

This was a team of Ashington Colliery workers from 1907 that went by the grand title of Ashington Albion. Back row: McDonald, Jack Miller, Joe Abercrombie, Billy Eastlake and Fred Waldock. Second back row: Will Taylor, John Guy, McMann, J. Taylor and Miller. Second front row: Lawrence, Jim Guy, F. Mordue, Billy Owens and George Thain. Front: Billy Dockerty, George Lawrence and Dalrymple.

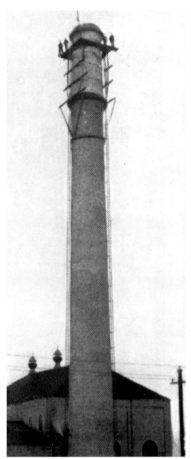

It was early in 1914 that it was decided to add another twenty-five feet to the already towering Ashington Colliery power station chimney. It was hooped by T. Reay of Stockton-on-Tees. Mr A. Paxton, the colliery's chief underground engineer, decided to make the ascent himself while the work was in progress – he had seen one of the men walking nonchalantly along one of the ordinary planks, which, as you will see in our photograph, were secured to the chimney by means of ropes. He probably thought that an ascent could be made easily enough. But where the stack curves out at what was formerly its peak, he found it a 'bit ticklish', he said, to get any further. He pointed out to a man on the job that the ropes securing the planks were shifting. 'Oh, that's nowt,' said the workman, 'they slipped six inches when Aa got on to them this mornin'.' The tall stack did sway a little – even more so when there was a wind. The Ashington officials seen at the base of the chimney are, far right back row: J. Bainbridge; in front from left: James Tait of Lynemouth, A. Paxton and Harry Oliver. The two men top left were private workmen.

Hospital and Infirmary, Ashington.

Ashington Hospital had its roots in the suffering and hardships of the miners in the town. In the nineteenth century if an accident happened down the pit, the victim was brought home and left to the care and limited skill of family and neighbours.

The men paid into the Ashington Fatal Accident Fund, making money available to pay capable women to assist in nursing injured miners. One step forward was the formation of a Nursing Association, again supported by regular contributions from the men. In 1910 this latter group decided that more medical services were needed in Ashington, and plans were laid for the building of a hospital. Delays in decision making meant that it was 1913 before the foundation stone was laid. This is a photo of the Hospital Infirmary as it was called shortly after 1914.

James Noble, at the age of eighty-two, writing in the *Ashington Advertiser*, said:

'The idea came to us when a group of men met one Sunday morning. We felt that Ashington needed a hospital and that something should be done about it. A planner called George Beattie from Wallsend offered his services for free, and each colliery in the district sent men daily to help where they could. Eventually, the day came to open the hospital and we were all there. Mr Ebby Edwards made a speech … and I said "all we need now is a doctor." We got one, built him a house and fixed his salary.'

Not much was known of what went on behind the closed doors of the Laboratory at Ashington Colliery. Let Ken Campbell explain: 'I applied for a job at the Lab, after I left Stanley Cook the grocer in North Seaton Road. I was surprised when I got a letter inviting me to attend the Lab – that was in 1935. The staff in 1947 consisted of those in this photo. The girls at the back were Ivy Scott, Joan Duff, Jean Hindhaugh, Marjorie Dunnet and Mary Drysdale. The boffins were George Arrowsmith, Nelson Conn, Wilson Reed, Dr Ainsley Crawford, Charlie Sewell, Jack Coxon, Tom Chicken with myself Ken Campbell on right.

'As well as analytical work on coal, mine air, mine dust and water we took samples from cows' milk from the colliery farms. That was a popular job, and we always insisted that pint bottles be sent, and the coffee that day was guaranteed to taste better than any the pit canteen made.

'Dr Crawford was highly respected by the Company directors and, I suspect, was held somewhat in awe by all who saw him arrive at the Lab in his 'Invicta' sports saloon, and wearing his ever-present bowler hat. The Lab was situated on the site of the old Duke Pit boiler house, just off the office square; the storehouse was at the front and the steps to the Duke heapstead at the rear. A notice on the front door said 'No Admittance'.'

The back streets of Ashington were covered in a web of railway tracks. This two-foot gauge rail was to carry the coal bogeys that delivered coal to the houses, and it was also used for the midden cleaners at night. This is a 1919 Peace Celebration Party in the back street of one of the 'top-end' rows. The track can be seen on the left.

On January 5th 1920 in the Priestman Memorial Hall (which was really two houses knocked together at the end of the Second Row, Ashington), there began a scheme of specialised training for would-be colliery officials. It was established by the ACC in conjunction with Northumberland County Education Department. It was to prepare young men to fill responsible posts in coal mining.

The school opened with fifteen students under a single teacher, Mr J. Gray, who was to see the scheme grow, move into new premises in Darnley Road in 1931, and ultimately retire as Principal of the Ashington County Mining School in 1942. This school was the forerunner of Northumberland College.

Many of these 1928 students ended up with distinguished careers. Back row: Stanley Hall, Frank Bell, F. Lemin, Tom Lockhart, Reuben Little and Clarence Bruce. Middle: John E Bridge, Len Finlay, John L. Wallace, Edward J. Dunn, George Hogg and Jimmy Anderson. Front row: John B. Floyd, Tim Brown, Mr J. Hodgson teacher, Fred Booth OBE mine manager, Mr J. Murray headteacher, Jim Cutter and Joe Thompson.

Who is he?

He started his football career by kicking a sixpenny ball about at the pit top of Northumberland's Ashington Colliery — but at the age of 16 he was playing for Newcastle United! Now 25, he was capped for England against Ireland in 1948, went to Rio two years later with the England touring team, and scored two brilliant winning goals for Newcastle in the 1951 Cup Final. Yes — it's Jackie Milburn!

The world didn't know it in 1938, but this young Hirst East schoolboy was destined for greater things, including the TV award of north-east personality of the last century. It is, of course, a young Jackie Milburn who had his name used by 'Quaker Oats' when they did an advert in 1951, the year that Wor Jackie scored two goals in Newcastle United's FA Cup Final win over Blackpool.

It was Jackie Milburn's turn to go back to school – the Mining School – during the Second World War. As a young apprentice fitter, Jackie went a couple of days a week to learn the theoretical side of engineering pitwork. This is a Youth Club group from 1943. Back: Bill Douglas, Joe Grieves, Bill Davison, Don Turner, Ray Bowart, John Straker, Bill Moran, Jack Milburn and Lenny Hay. Middle: Joe Smith, J. Wilson, Mary Cowan, Betty Thompson, Jean Cowan, Margaret Purdy, Nancy Hindhaugh, Betty Thompson, John Nixon and Les Moran. Front: Joyce Tomlin, Iris Lilley, Edna Henderson, Mary Skeen, Mr J. Harrison and his wife Edie, Dot Cutler, Margaret Richardson, Ivy Gibson and D. Wallace.

Many of these apprentices in 1941 went on to hold positions of importance in later life. Such as Bill Williams who started out at 14 years of age delivering oilcloth on a bike from Arrowsmith's shop on the Grand Corner. He said: 'I began at 7 am to light a coke-fired central heating boiler before the staff came in.' Bill later won a scholarship to go to Sunderland Technical College where he obtained his degree. Many years after serving his apprenticeship at Ashington Colliery, he was made Clerk of Works to oversee the sinking of Longhirst Drift in the 1950s. Bill later went to live in Wales where he was involved in the aftermath of the Aberfan disaster which claimed so many young lives. Photo shows back, left to right: Jimmy Tate, Alan Bell, George Strong, Dick Slaughter, Vince McCall, Bill Williams, Dave Thomas, Bobby York, Cecil Hogg, Chris Waddle, Jackie Tweddle. Front: unknown and Tommy Morgan.

Amazingly, Ashington miners, working at the biggest pit in Northumberland, were the last to have pit-head baths installed in 1952. They should have been built in the late 1920s, but the men thought that the ACC should put baths into their colliery houses, as they had done at Lynemouth. As was usual in the early days, the Coal Company won the day.

NATIONAL COAL BOARD
NORTHERN (N. & C.) DIVISION.

Ashington Colliery Pithead Baths
OPENING CEREMONY
On Saturday, 7th June, 1952.

J. JONES, Esq., M.B.E., Colliery Manager
will take the Chair at 11 a.m.

T. A. BENNETT, Esq., O.B.E., Secretary of the
Miners' Welfare Commission will hand over the
Buildings to the National Coal Board.

THE BATHS WILL BE DECLARED OPEN BY :
JAMES BOWMAN, Esq. Supported by R. MAIN, Esq.
Chairman of the Northern (N. & C.)　　General Secretary Northumberland
Divisional Coal Board.　　Area, National Union of Mineworkers

A Vote of Thanks will be proposed by GEORGE NELSON, Esq.
Branch Secretary, Ashington Lodge, National Union of Mineworkers

Seconded by D. HINDSON, Esq., M.C.,
Area General Manager, No. 3 Area.

The Baths will then be Opened, after which the Buildings may
be inspected by those present.

The Baths will be put into use on Monday, 9th June, 1952

On Saturday, 7th June, the Baths will be Open from 3 p.m. to
5 p.m. and Sunday, 8th June, 10 a.m. to 3 p.m. for inspection
by Workmen and Friends.

John Wilkinson, Printer, Ashington.

A 'Before and After' photo that shows how many changes can occur in thirty years. The top photo is of men leaving the Linton tankey that is standing on the right, crossing the line and making their way, running, to Station Bridge, Ashington. This is from the year 1908 – we know it was the Linton tankey because Ellington was not sunk until 1909. The photo below is from 1938 and now we see that a footbridge has been built over the line to make it safer to cross. And look at the massive pit-heap that has now risen in the background – you can accumulate a lot of pit waste in thirty years. But the most significant change is with the men themselves. No more in Jolson blackface; no more in filthy pit clothes. The miners who now used the Linton and Ellington tankeys to get them back home to Ashington, made full use of the pit-head baths at those two pits, and their wives would benefit too by not having to wash their pit 'claes' nor to scrub their husband's back in the tin bath by the fire.

Life for a pitman's wife in those days was a hard graft from morning till night. Here we see Margaret Ann 'Nan' Routledge about to throw a bowl of water over some bad lads outside her house in the Sixth Row. Her father 'Hoot' Gibson came from Stakeford where Nan was born in 1903. She often performed at the Fell 'em Doon Club as 'Black Mama'. She married Rattler Routledge and had five sons, Ronnie, Gibson, Robert, Laurence and Colin, and two daughters, Sheila and Margaret. Like most miners' wives, Nan has four pails of coals standing outside the back door and three bottles of milk to bring in.

And to prove that the pit-heaps were everywhere, we can see baby Sylvia Beattie in 1952 amid the pyrethrum and delphiniums in her father Michael's garden at New Moor Roadside Cottages in the shadow of yet one more mass of dross and shale. In any other book, this location might have been mistaken for the Swiss Alps, and that could be snow on the top of a mountain instead of white ash and smoke, belching from a pit-heap.

SECTION TWO

WOODHORN AND LINTON DRAW COALS, 1890s

Woodhorn Colliery

As coal production rose at Ashington Colliery so the coal workings moved further and further away from the shaft bottom. Needless time was wasted on getting 'inbye' (at the coal face). It was in 1894 that the Ashington Coal Company decided to open a new shaft at Woodhorn and a couple of years later at Linton, about two miles north. As there was no housing available at Linton at first, the men were housed in the Hirst area, and went to work on a pit tankey – an open-sided train.

When Woodhorn was first sunk, water kept seeping into the new shaft. This had to be pumped into barrels which were hauled to the surface. It was recorded on March 21st 1896: 'A Water Barrel in coming up the No 2 Shaft caught the pump and broke the ring of the chain, and fell to the bottom, breaking a flange of steam pipe.' On December 2nd 1896: 'James Rogers, a sinker, was killed by falling through the scaffold at Yard Seam No 2 Pit, whilst getting out of the kibble.'

The prices of the Hirst houses when built are real eye-openers. On October 1st 1897 an entry in the ACC log book states:

> J.&G. Douglas to build 76 flats on 38 sites in Sycamore Street with enclosed yard, for £119 19s a pair;
> To build 25 3-roomed cottages in Pont Street, £75 each;
> To build 25 4-roomed cottages in Mersey Street, £98 each.
> W.G. Gordon of Stakeford to build 27 4-roomed cottages in Laburnum Terrace for £93 10s.
> For cottages used in Medway Street use white bricks;
> For cottages built in Severn Street use red bricks.

Mersey was later absorbed into Milburn Road; Medway became Maple; and Severn was renamed Sycamore.

Here is an aerial view of the Hirst part of Ashington in 1928, rescued from a council tip by David Brown. In front are the 'Shakespearean' houses of Rosalind, Katherine, Portia and Juliet etc that lead on to Third Avenue. Next comes the Park School with part of what became St Andrew's Church on right. That white stuff emanating from the open ground is dust from an ash tip that later became the Hirst Park. Houses on the left are part of Ariel Street, but now the gaps have been filled in. Way over to the left is Welfare Crescent and Mary Gair's shop. The shrubbery, back centre, is the Hirst Flower Park where you can just spot the Miners' Memorial statue. Top right are the houses of South Villas which have now been replaced by the council houses of Broomlee and Sweethope Avenue etc. And those allotments, back centre, next to Alexandra Road, were eventually taken over to build prefabs during the Second World War.

And in the 1960s this is another way of looking at the Hirst, this time from the now-defunct United bus station on Woodhorn Road looking south. You can see the buses, front centre, with the Wallaw Cinema to the right. Spot the Arcade and Co-op buildings. To the right runs North Seaton Road which then forks at the Mortimer Club into Milburn Road, running past the Hirst North School and the Pavilion Theatre right down to the White Elephant. To the left, Hawthorn Road leads off from the Central Hall, passing St Andrew's Church and Hirst Park, all the way down to the South School and an emerging Tech College, next to Wembley Field. But aren't the streets all so regimented and boring. And yet the ACC named all these colliery raas after trees: Laburnum, Myrtle, Poplar, Sycamore, Maple and Chestnut, but you will be hard pressed to spot even a hanging basket here, let alone a tree.

The building of houses failed to keep up with the influx of workers from every part of Britain. Irishmen and their families abandoned their native land when a potato famine left them starving; tin miners came into the region from Cornwall; lead miners came across from Cumberland; as the Durham coalfield was worked out, so many moved into Northumberland. The Ashington Coal Company found work for them all.

Some Woodhorn Colliery men are seen here from around 1903. From left: unknown, Middlemiss, Lyall, Dick Williams who answered to his nickname of Whistler Dick, next Joe Lumb and Roger Wilson.

Woodhorn Colliery, *circa* 1910. Most of the men are wearing the cut-down short trousers of a typical hewer. A bridge over the railway line was built at a later date. Except for the two chimneys, this particular view is almost identical to the one you can see now at Woodhorn Colliery Museum.

Linton Colliery.

Joseph Chester (right) wrote: 'When I came to Linton in 1894, the civil parish of Ellington was then a rural one up to the hilt, and Linton was a desolate place indeed. There were only about twelve new colliery houses, four of which were occupied. There was nothing that one could call a road into or out of the colliery, except for the railway line on which ran a small tankey to convey the miners to and from Ashington at the beginning and ending of their day's work. Sinking operations had not yet begun at Linton. At Woodhorn, sinking operations were going on, but the likes of Ellington Colliery was in its dream stage and Lynemouth model village was, of course, a thing yet to be.'

Soon Linton Colliery was to fill the first railway wagon capable of holding 40 tons of coal. It is seen here in 1906 in the colliery yard. Some men (invisible to the naked eye) lined the track near the weigh cabin. John Noble who later became foreman blacksmith at Ellington; John Thirtle; Alexander Baxter, a deputy at Linton; Henry Wright; man with arms folded is Percy Beresford who emigrated to Canada; finally Joseph Gibson on right, a truckweighman and father of William Gibson who later became manager at Lynemouth.

The Linton Junior team of 1908. Back row: Wm Wood, who became master shifter at Linton, Alf Chester electrician, F.W. Ross enginewright at Old Moor who died in 1923, Thomas Fornear Linton  overman, Edwin Chester Linton cashier, William Fornear Linton deputy, and F. Bell who went to work at Birtley. Middle row: Thomas Bell, George R. Strong head rolleywayman, Bill Swanson, Joe Cracket who became a newsagent in Windsor Road, Newbiggin, Bob Wade of Woodhorn Colliery Office, and in front is Bill Hindmarsh.

This is the Linton Schoolboys football team of 1930. Back left is Edwin Harrison the headmaster, then Dolly Saunders, unknown, unknown, Fred Newman, Oliver, unknown, unknown, unknown. Front: unknown, unknown, Ernie Griffiths, Watson 'Watty' Thornton. Kneeling with ball is Farrington. Some not named could be Donnisons. Watty Thornton had an illustrious career as a footballer, coming back to play for Linton in the 1950s.

A group of Linton Blacksmiths before the Second World War. Second from left in back row is George 'Popeye' Mains, so called because of his liking for a clay pipe; he was the father of Pat Mains who managed Callers furniture shop in Ashington in the 1960s. One other man we know on photo is Tommy Renner who lived in Ashington in the street below the 'Piv'.

Britain went to war with Germany in 1914 and the local miners heeded the call to arms, signing up in their thousands. Five hundred Woodhorn Colliery men enlisted, including their manager, Mr Milburn and a future manager, Col

ASHINGTON RESERVISTS FOR THE FRONT. 13 J.T.B.

A.S.E. Richards. Milburn returned with a war wound that left him reliant on a stick for the rest of his life. Hundreds of local men failed to return at all. Their names were engraved on plaques and placed on the inside wall of the new Ashington Hospital and Infirmary which had only begun to be built at the outset of the war. The first patients were soldiers wounded and maimed in France. Some of them were probably on our photo that shows the unsuspecting miners lined up on the platform at Ashington Railway Station, prior to be posted abroad in 1916.

At around 8 am August 13th 1916, the Hospital staff braced themselves as word seeped through that a number of casualties were expected imminently. There had been a gas explosion at Woodhorn Colliery, and it soon became apparent that the new hospital had a major disaster on its hands. Thirteen men were killed.

This is how Nance Walton described that fateful Sunday:
'We were all getting ready for nine o'clock Mass when our neighbour, Mrs Hamilton, came in. 'Is your Ned at work this mornin'?' she asked mother. 'Aye,' me mother said. 'How's that, like?' The woman lowered her eyes: 'Oh, Aa just wondered.' She knew, you see, but she didn't want to let on. There was a colliery polis lived at the top of Chestnut Street then, and he eventually brought the word about the accident. By then me mother was on her way to the pit – we'd all heard about the explosion, you see. We never did get to church that Sunday.'

Proposed Woodhorn Memorial.

ELLINGTON COLLIERY SUNK, 1909

As the coal seams of Woodhorn edged nearer and nearer to the sea, it was thought that a new pit shaft needed to be sunk near the shore. And so it came about in 1909 that Ellington 'Betty' shaft was sunk. It was usual then to name pits after the daughters of coalowners. Betty was the daughter of Francis Priestman. Some of the first men who went to work at Ellington had previously been at Woodhorn Colliery. These included Robert Robson a hewer of Woodhorn Road; George Richardson, age 29, East Hawthorn Road; Bill Straughan, age 14, driver, 79 Portia Street; and Richard Wigham, age 27, Ellesmere, Stakeford. One of the first men to work at Ellington was Johnnie T. Rowe who had previously been to America.

The St John Ambulance Brigade was always a prominent feature of the ACC, each of the pits having their own Corps. Here we have a simulated accident on Ellington platform in 1914. Some of the men are Arthur Richardson, Joe Lambert, Kit Barrass, Joe Page, Harry Adams and Adam Hudson. The old tankey has been decorated with the name 'Ashington' on the side.

Bill Johnstone, now living in Canada, was working at Ellington Colliery as a putter when the 1926 Strike ended. Here he relates some of his story.

'The social gap between the manager of a colliery and the miner in those days was so wide it could not be bridged. In the seven years that I spent at Ellington Pit I saw the manager once. He walked past me in company with another official without a hint of recognition. As for the coalowners, they lived on their vast estates, in their manor houses and castles, as far removed from their workmen as the stars in the sky.

(Unlike the men and boys) 'The pit ponies at Ellington were well catered for. Each had its own stall in a warm, electrically lit stable. They were washed down at the end of each shift, fed chopped hay, carrots and grain, and bedded down in clean peat moss. The story that pit ponies were blind when they were brought to the surface is a fallacy. The ponies relied on the light of pit lamps, and their stables were lit at all times. As a result, their eyes were accustomed to light and darkness the same as any other underground worker.

'On an average day a putter could take care of five or six hewers. His wages were based on the number of tubs he handled. In the advance longwall system of mining at Ellington, the haulage roads that the putter used were maintained through the 'gob' – an area from which the coal had been extracted, sometimes referred to as the 'goaf'. As a result he worked in the newly mined-out places where subsidence was not complete. Consequently, the roof and floor were continually on the move. It was not uncommon to take an empty tub to a miner, and when fetching it out fifteen minutes later find that the roof had settled a few inches, making it impossible to get the tub through until a wooden prop had been chopped out or roof taken down to make the needed height.'

Both now in their nineties, Bill Johnstone and his wife Dorothy are seen in this 1998 photo.

Like the Linton workers, Ellington miners originally lived in Ashington and had to be ferried by tankey, seen here under one of the few bridges built over the track. A similar one was to be built when Lynemouth Colliery got underway.

The Ellington miners lost no time in getting up a football team. This squad from 1910 has front row: John Holland, Lawrence Bell under-manager, Jos Aspin later killed in action. Middle row: C.G. Wood who emigrated to South Africa, Joseph Bell winding engineman, I. Robinson who went to South Africa, T. Johnson deputy, W. Wright who went to Australia. Back row: Joseph Wood powderman, G.D. Mavin, A. Storey went to Australia, Robert Gustard under-manager at Linton, T. Stamp of Moorhouse Farm, R. Stamp, and H. Aspin killed in action.

Arthur Hendy came up with his Cornish family at the turn of the century. His father was William Summer Hendy who became a county councillor and was heavily involved in miners' union affairs. The family lived in Richardson Street and later Katherine Street. Arthur had three sisters: Doris, Nellie and Elsie who married Harry Wilkinson who worked at Ashington Colliery. The photo shows a group of Ellington Joiners in 1918 with a 14-year-old Arthur Hendy in front centre holding circular saw. Like so many other pitmen, Arthur suffered a severe accident at his job. It was while working on the winding wheel at Ellington – someone set it away while Arthur was still on it – and as a result, his arm was disfigured for the rest of his life. Arthur came to live in Newbiggin from 1930 until he died in 1981.

THE WELFARE SCHEME, 1926 STOPPAGE AND 'OUT CLUBBIN'

In 1920, under the Factories Act, it became compulsory for employers to provide social amenities for their workers. The Ashington Coal Company is always being praised for the way in which it 'took care of its men'. But under close scrutiny it can be seen that the ACC had to have its arm twisted by government legislation before it acted. Individual Welfare facilities were set up at Ashington Institute, the Recreation Ground, Hirst Welfare, Ellington and Linton. When Lynemouth Village was built in the early 1920s, it too was able to take advantage of a marvellous Institute and extensive playing fields. By far the most popular sport was football, and the Ashington Welfare League was soon running three leagues for seniors, juniors and midgets (under sixteens). This photo was captured in front of Ashington Colliery's wooden heapstead, with towering chimneys in the background, showing ten of the junior teams (16-18) all wearing brand-new strips.

Many of the early football teams in the league took their names from where they worked. This is the winning Loco United from 1928. Back row: J. Irving, George Reed, J. Gardner, Norman Johnson, P. Atkinson, J. Sawkill, G. Robson and J. Reed. Front row: J. Thompson, J. Davison, R. Davison, S. Redfearn, T. Charlton, J. Gillon and F. Bell.

Rugby in Ashington took place mainly on the Rec, and to reach the ground you had to traverse a bridge over the railtrack of the colliery yard. This 1930 squad back row: A. Clark, G. Leech, R. Bell, A. Smith, J.O. Gairdner son of Frank Gairdner first hospital superintendent, R. Patterson and R. Elliott. Middle row: H Clarke, James Leslie Brownrigg one of the original Pitmen Painters, Percy Bates, C. Goldsmith, Maurice Abbott and J. Noble. Front row: G. Wiseman and J. Watson.

The Welfare football league attracted some pitmen teams who were loyal to their churches. This particular squad represented St Aidan's RC Church and won the title in 1930. The two trainers are R. Rogers and J. Rowley, club secretary Will Carey is seated left with Father Coyle on right. The team was M. Mahon in goal, Dan Parry and W. Dillon fullbacks, W. Campbell, E. Reilly and S. Nuttall as halfbacks, and forwards were Billy Gaines, G. Conroy, Joe Conroy, Billy Clark and Joe Cain.

The game of hockey was popular among the pitmen and their ladies, as can be seen from this large squad of players in 1927. Ed Gladson, bottom right, a pit onsetter, played right on until his fifties.

This is the Ashington Collieries Welfare Tennis Team of 1934 that won the 'E' Division of the County, seen here at the Rec. Back left is Andy Dixon who was also a fine footballer, then K. Hindmarsh and W.D. Lytham. Front left is J. Bolton, then C. Goldsmith, A.S. Crow and George Hewitt. One member absent was F. Aitchison.

Will Robson drew some great illustrations for the *Ashington Colliery Magazine* from which the majority of these details are taken. Here is his 1934 impression of what the average pitman should be doing in his spare time: heading straight for the Welfare Sports Club.

Of course the Welfare Scheme did not run itself. It needed dedicated men who would give up their spare time to organise events. These men were on the Welfare Football Management Committee. Back row: Bob Gilholme, George Hall, R. Prior, George Clementson also a boxing coach, J. Foster, J. Colman

and F. Brodie. Front row: A. Lackenby, T. Atkinson, Dickie Howe secretary, Frank Bradley chairman, J.W. Brodie, R. Darling and H. Bebbington.

One young lady who did a stint at Ashington Pit Canteen was Jenny Riches (Mrs Liddell). She said: 'When the second war began, I went to stay with my mother, taking my young son Tommy. Financially, things were not good so I decided I would have to get a job. At that time Commander Kemp was in charge of the Welfare Department at Ashington

This is inside Ashington Canteen in 1938 – the man on left is Tom Hunter who was a lodger of man next to him, Jimmy Drysdale; man sitting on right is Mick Drysdale.

Colliery, running it with Dickie Howe and Fred Reed, the Ashington poet. It was Kemp who chose the ladies who would work in the pit canteen. And that was where I went.

'Charlie Sewell was the manager at first, but he was close to retiring age. He and I got on famously – he had a wry sense of humour. The old canteen was a two-storey building, stores downstairs and canteen upstairs. It was heated by a huge black metal stove on which we boiled all the water for tea, washing up and cleaning. The canteen had a cement floor on which we sprinkled sand, then used a broom to get rid of all the dirt and grease that came from the men's boots and clothes. I had to close the canteen at 5 pm until this was accomplished.

'Charlie Sewell retired after about a year and I was put in charge. There were four girls working there then: Betty Bell, Mary Hindhaugh, Nancy Ruddick and another Mary, and there was usually a young lad helping out, a trainee or an apprentice.

'Friday was the highlight for both miners and staff – it was payday – which for me meant about two pounds a week. This is a 'set' of miners in 1938 waiting outside the Canteen on a payday Friday morning, and only one without a flat cap.'

'Most of the colliers were in what they called 'sets', and the leader was paid for the whole team. So the money had to be changed in the canteen and shared out, or 'settled-up' as it was called. Most of our customers never carried any money, so they were put on our 'tick-list'. But they always paid their debts. They were like Musketeers: all for one and one for all, and were the wittiest people I ever worked with.'

'Later I became the colliery telephonist, and this is me at my switchboard.'

Anticipating the building of pit-head baths in 1923, this is what cartoonist David Barton saw as the 'before and after' on the pit tankey after the baths were built.

A minority sport played by the miners was table tennis with tables at the Rec and Hirst Welfare. Here we have a squad getting ready in one of the Rec dressing rooms prior to a game. Back, from left: George Redpath, a former stoneman in the Bothal Pit; Bob Smith used to live in New Moor Cottages; Billy Pyle whose father was Sexton at the  Holy Sepulchre when the family lived above the church hall; Les Redpath, the best ping-pong player that year, excelling at most sports, brother of George, Les was a fitter before moving down south; Raymond Sewell went into mechanical engineering, ending up as Group Engineer, this in spite of being torpedoed in the Second World War; Jimmy Anderson, a master weighman on bank at Ashington Colliery for over twenty years before working underground at Ellington Colliery; Jimmy Grieves, an NCB tankey driver, very involved in all kinds of sports. Others who played table tennis at the time included Bill Clyde, Bill Dixon, Walter Burrell, Norman Dunn, W. Foster, Raymond Scott, Clarke Floyd and Billy Bolam who lived in the 10th Row with brother George. Last two on right not known.

But it was always the game of football that dominated the miners' conversation. 'Hoo did the Toon get on on Sa'da?' was a favourite question in foreshift on a Monday, or 'Did the Colliers dee all right at the weekend?' when enquiring about Ashington FC's exploits, who  were in the Football League in the 1920s. This photo shows a home game at Portland Park when the Colliers entertained their neighbours Blyth Spartans in a North Eastern League game on New Year's Day 1921. There was a huge crowd of 7,140, as you can see from this photo taken from the west side of the ground. That grandstand carried advertising on the roof for 'Blacklock's Department Store' which later became 'Doggarts', on Station Road.

Early Pit Stoppages

Coalmining and trade disputes have gone hand-in-hand since the first pit shaft was sunk. In 1926 during the Stoppage Will Robson saw the funny side of things with this cartoon.

"A strike's aalreet, but by gum Aa wad rather be at work."

Soup kitchens were set up for the miners' children. Like this one at Linton School not long after the school had opened.

Back To Work and Play

After the long stoppage of 1926, it was back to work as before. New workshops were built at Ashington Colliery; the scene in the above photo is almost blotted out by a puff of steam from a passing tankey. The other photo shows a group of men who helped to build the new structure. Sadly we have no names for this group captured on camera by Ross Miles, an Ashington historian to whom we are greatly indebted for the way he dedicated his life to keeping alive the heritage of the area.

For those too young to take part in organised sport, there was always the newly-built playgrounds at the Rec and Hirst Welfare. Rides were featured with names like Plank Swings and See-Saws, Pirate Ships and Giant Slides. I remember going to the Hirst Welfare playground as a child – we called it the Ha'penny Park, as that was the price of admission. The 25ft high slide was later dismantled as a child fell from the top and was killed.

For recreation, the veterans could attend their very own hut. This is the forerunner of what is now the Veterans' Hut behind Woodhorn Road. What a run-down shack this looks with its bare boards and rough-hewn cupboard on the left. The man in bowler hat, second from the right at the front, is Andrew Murray, a Scot who came down from The Plashetts to work at Ashington Colliery and live at No 89 Beatrice Street.

It was literally a dark day for many newcomers to the district when they were drafted in to help out in the pits belonging to the Ashington Coal Company. It was in December 1943 that Ernest Bevin, then Minister of Labour, decreed that one out of every ten men who enlisted for the forces should go instead to one of the nation's coalmines. What a culture shock for the likes of Ron Keene, seen on the right of this photo. Ron was born in 1925 and brought up in the London borough of Hendon. After passing his scholarship, Ron went on to grammar school and then a position with the Inland Revenue. Like most patriotic citizens, Ron signed up for military service on the day of his eighteenth birthday. 'Imagine my disbelief,' said Ron, 'when I was told that I had been selected for conscription to the mines, from the first ballot of names.' Ron is seen here outside the Miners' Hostel that stood next to Ashington's Central Hall. Man on left is Vic Sampson of East London, and in centre is Alex Foster of Greenock.

And talking of the Central Hall … the local miners were great lovers of good music. And that is certainly what they got every Sunday evening during the celebrity concert season that took place there from the 1930s until it was so brutally and needlessly

demolished. Mister Music-man was Normanton Barron, on left, who was responsible for bringing many famous singers and musicians to the area. Next to him is Miss Audrey Stimpson who was equally well-known and loved for her dedication to the teaching of music. Audrey, a teacher at many local schools, was the first Head of Music at Hirst High School when it opened in 1974. This photo from the early 1960s shows that another Ashington lass, opera singer Maureen Williams, far right, was also on the bill that night.

Pubs and Workingmen's Clubs open their Doors

In his informative book *Opening Time*, Jack Leslie tells us that the Portland Arms Hotel was granted a licence in September 1890, and that two of the early licensees were Thomas Forbes and Sylvester Strong. But the name that local folk still attach to the Portland is that of Bill Kell senior and his son Bill who, with his red-headed wife Rusty, built up a reputation for good ale and good order from the post-war years right up to the '60s. Old Bill Kell is seen here on the steps of the Portland, feeding the horse ridden by a well-known character, Fred Curry.

One of Ashington's characters was Jack Hamilton, of the trilby hat and red nose. He is seen here on left with young Bill Kell and Geordie Thorborn in the early 1950s.

A licence for the Grand Hotel, seen here in the photo at the turn of the twentieth century, was granted in 1893, and to the North Seaton Hotel (now the Elephant) in 1901. But it was the speed of the mushrooming social clubs that caught everyone unawares. Two clubs, the West End and the New Hirst (Mortimer) vied for which one should be the first to serve ale. Officially, the New Hirst won when they opened their doors on November 17th 1901, while the West End took their first orders a few weeks later in December of that year.

The clubs soon became affiliated to the Federation Breweries. This is a 1928 Hospital Carnival float, telling the folks that it only cost six pounds for a barrel of their beer. Man in centre in trilby is George Mather who was Federation Chairman at the time as well as holding many other major positions in Ashington.

The Social Clubs ran their own football teams in the Welfare League. There were lots of pitmen in this great team that played for the Hirst Universal in the early 1940s; many of these men were good enough to turn out for Ashington FC reserves, such as Dickie Ellis front centre and next to him Peasy Emery, while second right at back is a no-nonsense tackler Peter Merryweather.

Sports Personalities of 1958 were invited to the Premier Club to receive awards. Ashington's Mr Football, George Cave, is extreme left; others featured are Hirst East End men, Ernie Chartlon and Jim Slaughter; at back second left is Hylton

Laing a director of Ashington FC and Gateshead; top right was one of the judges, Joe Keagan; back second right is Bill Ward who started off Bedlington Mechanics, a joiner at Bedlington 'D' Pit; and centre back is the young lad who won the title Sports Personality of 1958, an Ashington fitter who went on to take the billiard world by storm, John Sinclair.

It was back to the Premier Club in 1963 for a presentation to boxing champion Maurice Cullen, a former Durham miner, seen on left. Next is long-serving club secretary John Riddell, Billy Eastlake chairman, local boxer Tommy Todd, and Edwin Straker the Premier's treasurer. Maurice had left his car outside the club on Woodhorn Road, but an over-zealous policeman stuck a parking ticket on the vehicle. However, Tommy Todd used his influence and persuaded the bobby that he was being a bit too harsh on the champ who had brought his Londsdale Belt to put on display.

A favourite part of club-going was to be entertained by a Go-as-you-Please, a sort of talent show. Usually about eight or ten acts took part, some of the entertainers went from club to club doing nothing else but taking part in these shows. One lad who was just in it for the beer was John Ellison, a local paper seller. John often took to the stage at the Comrades Club, and had the joint jumping with his rendition of 'When the Saints go Marching in' on his faithful mouth-organ. Illustration by Len Hay.

Members of a club formed themselves into 'Gleemen', and went around to other clubs and old people's homes entertaining. This is a 1950s group at the West End Club. Concert chairman Jack Wallace is leaning on piano, far right.

In December 1986 it was the turn of the Linton & Woodhorn Club to hand out Certificates of Merit to member Perry Clough who also received a wallet of notes and his wife, Gwen, a carriage clock. From left: John Bell club chairman, Harry Drysdale, Gwen and Perry Clough, Willie Cairns secretary, Ernie Moore and Tommy Burns, branch EC member.

Fell 'em Doon Club awarded prizes in the 1970s to the members of their Rose
Show. From left: J. Coombs, Ernie Moore, Councillor Jack Mather, Harry
Drysdale, J. Summers, M. Cook, J. Davison and Will Coombs, the judge of the
show.

A contest for Miss Clubland was won by Miss Jacqueline Scott from the Hirst
Premier, while Mrs Olly Allsopp of Pegswood became the most Glamorous
Grannie of 1973. Left: Jimmy Lynam secretary of Northumberland CIU, Miss
Scott, Mrs Allsopp and Harry Drysdale branch chairman.

In the workingmen's clubs, leek growing and the name of Dickie Freeman went hand-in-hand. He was the man they all had to beat in the Leek Shows for over twenty years. And it wasn't only giant leeks that were Dickie's forté – he won many prizes for his stands of mixed vegetables. 'And what's that like for a stick o' celery?' he is asking Joe Conroy and Alec Moore, two of the members at the Universal Club in 1960.

A fairly recent photo of the Hirst Progressive Leek Show in September 1996. For Brian Henderson, centre, it was success three times in a row. It was a family trait to grow big leeks because Brian's father had also won many prizes. However, the prize for Best Leek of the Show went to young David

Brainbridge, son of the club treasurer, Bill. Handing over the shield is club chairman, Elly Turnbull who works at Alcan. Elly at that time had a record of running in ten consecutive Great North Runs in aid of Charity.

LYNEMOUTH
A MECHANICAL PIT, 1934

Lynemouth Colliery had been used by the ACC since the 1920s, but coal had been drawn from Ellington Pit. The colliery houses of Lynemouth were being built during the 1926 Stoppage together with the Institute and Welfare facilities. But it was not until 1934 that Lynemouth Colliery was able to stand alone and it quickly became successful because of the new technology used in extracting the coal.

Alan Robson, *Colliery Magazine* editor, wrote in July 1934:

Today I went on a country walk, past the old Mill at Woodhorn Village, and along a beautiful new road which marches parallel with the North Sea. And anon I came to some brand-new buildings, a huge collection of brick, concrete and steel. A steel framework enclosed a couple of wheels – the sign manual of a colliery. Another structure was surmounted by something that looked like a sugar bowl. I am told that they wash coal in this contraption.

I went inside the long building known as the Screens. By the time the coal arrives here it has been washed, watered, cleaned and graded. This new pit is called Lynemouth. Many people have given a lot of thought before the colliery took place. There doesn't seem to be a lot of men working on the heapstead – it seems to be all mechanical. But when you do meet some chaps in the office, lamp room, screens or wherever, I was struck by the number of smiling faces. I fancy it comes with the coals. Anyhow, it is a valuable asset and one which should produce good results. One of the workers made a remark which explains the whole thing: 'Aye, we're just one big happy family, here.'

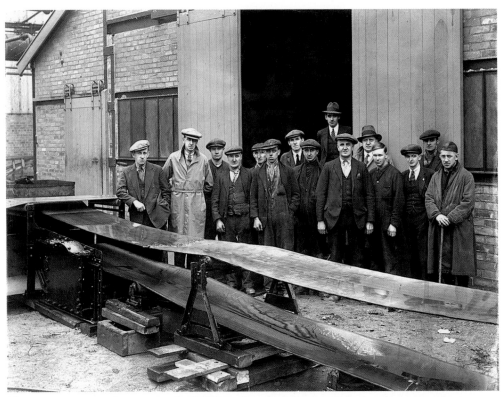

First conveyor at Lynemouth Colliery in 1934 was put in by the manufacturers Hugh Wood – that is he in trilby fifth right at back. Colliery manager Bill Gibson is far right next to a youthful Ross Miles. Far left is Mr Richardson and George Conway, Dick Ross and two cousins both called Bill Ramsay.

A major reconstruction scheme took place at Lynemouth between 1949 and 1957, and, as a result, the saleable output was raised from 1,000 tons to almost 6,000 tons per day. Coal production became highly mechanised, and there were substantial reserves of coal up to 13 feet in thickness in the undersea area of the combined High Main and Main Seams. Top photo shows work underway in the pit-yard – in the distance can be seen a row of Ellington council houses. Second from top shows the east side of the yard where work is starting on the coal bunkers – the road twists around into Cresswell. The next photo is a view of the old road that used to run past the colliery – this is now a cyclepath. Bottom photo is a general view of Lynemouth Colliery with the timber yard in foreground.

Colliery mechanics were among the best-trained and skilful in the land. Here we see two groups of Lynemouth mechanics in the 1950s. One is a group of optimistic gamblers about to catch their bus to Ayr races. Norman Campbell who supplied both photos is the tall man in rear centre wearing glasses.

Most colliery groups whether they be deputies, mechanics, surveyors etc, had their own special annual get-togethers for either an outing or a sit-down meal. Here we see many of the same Lynemouth mechanics posing outside the Old Ship at Newbiggin. Little did any of them realise that their livelihood – and that of almost 2,000 of their colleagues – was about to be threatened by an underground fire.

The title of 1958 Lynemouth Apprentice of the Year was won by Billy Lyall of Newbiggin. He is seen here been given his award by Raymond Sewell, group engineer, at the first annual dinner of the Lynemouth Branch of the Colliery Mechanics Union. George Down, branch secretary, is on left, with Billy Milne and Gilly Jobling far right. The event was held in Grand Hotel, and Billy was quite unaware of what was

happening. The cup was a memorial to Billy Marsh, an electrical engineer who worked at Lynemouth for 24 years who had died suddenly the year before. Raymond Sewell said: 'Billy Lyall has been chosen out of a total of 43 eligible apprentices. The idea of an award has come from the mechanics themselves, and I think this annual contest will become an inspiration to young apprentices.'

Two years later it was the turn of another Newbiggin man, nineteen-year-old Ronnie Robinson, to lift the glittering prize. He is seen here receiving the cup from Lynemouth manager, Mr A.Z. Lang, in the Trade Union Hall. Mr Lang told his audience of colliery craftsmen and union officials that it was always a pleasure to make an award to someone who had worked so hard. He said: 'We are often hearing that coal is dying. Don't you believe it. As far as we at Lynemouth are concerned, there is a tremendous amount of scope in the Industry.'

Mr H. Sambrook, Lynemouth electrical engineer, said there were many facilities available for young people today. Mr J. Leatham, Area General Secretary of Mechanics' Union, said it was up to anyone with ambition to take advantage of the education provided by the NCB.

Two veterans with over fifty years service to the mines were also awarded certificates, these were James Foster, of 13 Council Terrace, and W.J. Reay, 13 Woodhorn Road, Newbiggin. Mr John Dobbin, chairman of Lynemouth Mechanics' Association, was in the chair for the evening. All those named are featured on our photo, taken by Jack Laws, in January 1960.

Fire at Lynemouth Colliery, 1966
by Frank Ramsay

'I left the Durham & Northumberland Mines Rescue Brigade in 1953 to take up my post as Fire Officer at Woodhorn Colliery. One of my main duties was to inspect the Safety Escape Road from Lynemouth to Woodhorn, every week. I arranged for transport to convey me back to Woodhorn Colliery by road. So I had an insight into some of Lynemouth's many problems – let's say I was not much impressed by the management outlook – it appeared that production was their only priority, with safety matters being a necessary burden.

'In May 1964 I was appointed Area Fire Officer (my son Peter, also a rescue brigadesman took over my duties at Woodhorn). He followed my advice and kept a wary eye on Lynemouth's development.

'The colliery was also to be a showpiece. Every new piece of mining equipment was installed; the colliery yard was laid out with tarmac roads, trees and shrubs, flower beds, even hanging baskets for the office block. The planners may have got it right with Lynemouth Village and colliery yard, but they sited the shafts in the worst possible place. They holed into Woodhorn Colliery's old Yard Seam workings. They made numerous attempts to seal off these old workings, but finally decided to open up and remodel these old roadways and make an Escape Road into Woodhorn Colliery. It was then hoped that Lynemouth would develop five or six miles out to sea.

'Lynemouth Pit was also sunk in an area of volcanic faults – many seams of coal were not uniform, some dipping and rising. Some seams of coal were of the usual thickness as in other parts of the coalfield, but they also had seams from 18 to 20 feet thick. It was not only a coalmine, but in production eyes it was a goldmine!

This photo shows one of the Lynemouth underground roadways which was completely flooded, leaving behind thousands of pounds worth of mining cars and machinery. This put nearly 2,000 men out of work. Some of them took early retirement, some were absorbed by the local collieries. The Area Production figure went down by 19,000 tons per day.

'However, it was also endowed with endless trouble from sea water, methane gas and outbreaks of spontaneous combustion, which resulted in numerous outbreaks of fire. I had first visited Lynemouth Colliery in 1938 whilst a member of the Ashington Mines Rescue Brigade, but I was never very impressed with their safety standards with regards to Fire and Rescue.

'Over the years, Lynemouth had had many small fires, however, in 1966 they had an outbreak of fire on one of the two coal-faces. The labour force was withdrawn and Rescue Brigades from Ashington, Houghton-le-Spring and Benwell were quickly on the scene. As Area Fire Officer, I was also in attendance. After eleven days, the Brigade had to withdraw. It was a case of 'Everybody Out ... and Quick'. The powers-that-be decided to flood the shaft. It took fourteen days for the water to reach the shaft level.

'It wasn't very long before the bosses sharpened their pencils and came up with a plan to re-open Lynemouth Colliery, which, on paper, had millions of tons of coal reserves out under the North Sea. They sank the 1 in 4 Bewick Drift, approximately 1,000 yards to the north of No 1 Shaft which would hole into the high roadways, free of fire and free of water. They built new winding houses, offices, conveyor belt systems and stock yards. When the day came for the Drift to 'hole', I had arranged for the Rescue Brigade to accompany me into the re-opened roadways. They had holed exactly where they had planned, and, joy of joys, there was no fire or water.

'While all this had been going on, Ellington Colliery, two and a half miles to the north, had been driving an underground roadway towards Lynemouth Colliery. Up until then all of Ellington's 16,000 tons of coal per day was being transported by coal wagons along a private NCB railway into Lynemouth Washery. By driving this new underground roadway, Ellington Colliery's private line, plus six locos, staff, signal boxes etc, would become redundant – a saving of thousands of pounds a year. By linking Ellington Colliery and Lynemouth, it was to become known as the 'Ellington and Lynemouth Combine'. As can be imagined, this created problems with management: senior officials, ventilation officers etc. It also caused the safety department to have a 'think' as regards fire-risk, as now there would be well over 30,000 tons of coal daily en route to the Washery and Alcan Smelter.

'They created a new post: Unit Fire Officer, and I was promoted to this position, being *in situ* from 1968 until I retired through ill-health (arthritis) in August 1978. As a footnote, when I retired, Lynemouth's farthest coal face was almost eight miles out to sea, and Ellington was approaching Alnmouth Whin-Dyke.'

Photo shows Rescue Brigadesman Frank Ramsay second left, with Bill Burfield, George Fulthorpe and Jack Evans, attending Choppington Pit in 1948 to a gas explosion which claimed the life of a deputy called Jim Prime.

BLOOD ON THE COAL

HIRST PARK, ASHINGTON

Coalmining was always a dangerous occupation. A gas explosion at Woodhorn Colliery claimed the lives of thirteen men on August 13th 1916. They had gathered at the shaft at 6 am for a special shift, driving a new roadway. Within an hour there was an ignition of deadly methane gas sparked by a naked flame, leaving all the men dead or dying. At the subsequent inquest, a verdict of Accidental Death was given, but the miners still blamed poor management procedures. The memorial to the dead men, seen above, was erected in Hirst Park, but later moved to Woodhorn Colliery Museum.

From the Ashington Group of collieries, in one year alone, 1938, these nine men lost their lives underground at various local pits:

Robert McLean Hood, aged 27, of 46 Beatrice Street, Ashington. Employed at Linton Colliery as a stoneman.

George Ledgerwood, aged 31, of 12 Storey Crescent, Newbiggin. Was employed at Lynemouth Colliery as a composite worker.

James William Armstrong, aged 38, of 99 Juliet Street, Ashington. Employed as a chock-drawer at Ellington Colliery.

William Rutherford, aged 53, of 71 Fifth Row. Killed as a result of a fall of stone.

John William Newton, aged 32, a drawer at Ashington Colliery.

Obediah Self, aged 28, of 13a George Street. Killed while coalcutting at Woodhorn Pit.

James Rossiter, aged 67, of 11 Chestnut Street. A shaftsman for over 30 years.

Robert White, of Arundel Square, Ashington. Head horsekeeper died six weeks after an accident down Woodhorn Colliery.

Adam Scott, of St Andrew's Terrace, Ashington. A master wasteman, died as a result of pit accident at Woodhorn.

James Martin Bartle was only 26 when he was killed at Woodhorn Pit (above) in 1943. He was working in the Penker Seam. Jim was in foreshift filling when the putter came into his workplace asking for help as he was 'off the way'. Jim went to help, but was trapped when some coal came away and 'happed him up'.

Other miners died, like Archie Smith, killed at Ashington Colliery on Monday September 1st 1947. He was aged forty-three. Archie, a composite worker, was buried in a fall together with George Coils who was also killed. Archie's father died six weeks later, it was said from a 'broken' heart. The family then lived at No 54 Eighth Row, Ashington, where Archie was an expert bowls player, often turning out for Ashington Institute.

Bob Mitchell Stephen was killed at Ashington Colliery on May 26th 1950, trapped under a steel chute as he rode the belt outbye at the end of his shift. Another man, Gordon Renwick, was killed the same day in a separate accident.

Editor: My mother often took it into her head to 'shift hoose'. In 1947 we found ourselves living at No 67 Pont Street, Ashington. Next door were the Collins family which included daughter Jean. Young Jean was wed around this time to Joe Auld, and the couple moved in with Jean's mother, as so many other marriages began. As an impressionable 13-year-old lad, I remember Jean well as being an attractive girl. Jean and Joe are seen here after their wedding at St John's Seaton Hirst. About a year after this my mother decided on yet another move, this time to No 99 Maple Street. I lost touch with the Collins family after that until October 24th 1963.

Here we let Brian Auld, their son, take up the story: 'I was only sixteen and timber leading at New Moor on that particular day. I was supposed to go in at 7 am, but slept the caller and didn't get down till eight. I remember that my father had shouted up the stairs: "I'm off now, son." They were the last words I heard him say. Towards the end of my shift I was approached by a young overman called Hughie Orr who said I should report to the undermanager's office when I got to bank.

'On my way outbye I met the night-shift men coming in. Usually, there would be a bit banter as we passed each other on the roadway, but this time they just lowered their heads and walked past. It was Herbie Swinburne who gave me the news that my father had been killed. Herbie was one of the best pitmen I ever met.

'At the same time as my father had been killed, in another part of the Duke Pit a chap called Peter Appleby had been badly injured. By sheer coincidence, the Applebys lived next door to us at 67 Pont Street. Colliery officials must have been mixed up because someone went to the Appleby house at No 67, and told his wife that her husband Peter had been killed. Then he went next door to our house and told my mother that my father was all right but had been badly injured.

'The papers were full of it the next day with the headline: 'Tea-time Tragedy for Next Door Neighbours.' When the mistake was rectified, it was to our great loss and grief. This is part of a poem that I wrote about the incident:

> The very morning his life was taken
> he'd called me out of bed,
> grabbed his bait-bag, opened the door.
> "I'm off now, son," the last words he said.
> And I was the one to identify
> my mining father, now scrubbed clean.
> And he was a young man of just thirty-eight,
> and I, a mere boy of sixteen.'

Editor: The pages of this book are insufficient to name all the brave men who lost their lives down the five pits of the Ashington Group of Collieries. This is what Edna Hogg had to say: 'Bob Hogg (right) was only sixteen when we met. He was already a keen bandsman, playing tenor horn for the North Seaton Colliery Band. Later, when that pit closed, he played for the Ashington band.

'After we married, as was usual when he went to the pit, I waved him goodbye – it was 10 pm Tuesday June 18th 1969, and I never saw him again until he was brought home in a box. As part of a mechanisation team, he had to travel to all the collieries in the area. That particular week he was working at Lynemouth, three miles out under the sea.

'In the middle of the shift, he switched off the machine he was working on. But when he switched it on again, it was found to be 'in reverse', and Bob was jammed between that machine and another. The handle pierced his main artery and he bled to death.

'Not a penny compensation was paid as it was said to have been his own fault. He was forty-eight years old.'

Lynemouth Colliery.

To try to combat the high number of fatalities and serious accidents down the pit, the ACC employed Joe Dockerty as a full-time Safety Officer at Ashington. On this photo is the editor's father, Jack Kirkup, showing how to put a 'stay' prop in to prevent parts of the coal face from falling on the miner. It was taken in November 1937 in Ashington's Duke 5/4 Seam. Jack Kirkup gained his deputy overman's ticket a year later.

Chock-drawing was an important operation in conveyor filling. Joe Dockerty said: 'Where chocks have to be drawn and moved forward into a new position, it is not sound practice to draw them relying only on the ordinary timber, ie, props and planks behind you.' A miner's chant often heard at a football game was: 'Gan on Geordie – draaw the buggers chocks!' (Take his legs away).

First Aid training has enjoyed a long tradition in the mining industry which has always been a potentially dangerous occupation. As the years rolled on, laws were introduced to ensure that a minimum number of qualified first-aiders were in the mine whenever men were working.

Photo shows Lynemouth Senior team and Juniors from Ellington Colliery. From left: Wilf Dick, George Hanson, Alec Cummings, Jim Jeffries, Bill Clancey, Billy Barrass, Les Scott, Ernie Baker, Bob Wright and Tommy Thornton; seated right is Dr J. Dobson, area medical officer for the NCB in the 1950s.

This photo is of Lynemouth Colliery First Aid team of 1954. Back: John Freeman, Alan Youngs, Ron Staines (capt), Joe Hays, Tom Orr, Albert Rogers; seated left Horace Madeley, right Lynemouth colliery manager, Mr Sillitoe.

WARTIME BOOM
YEARS AND BEYOND

It is a fact that, whenever there was a war, then the
government of the day began to scream out for Coal.
The black diamonds were needed for so many vital
industries, as illustrated above in the *Ashington Colliery
Magazine* of November 1940.

Fred Reed, writing for the *Ashington Colliery Magazine*, published his own poem in 1940 called 'The Home Front', praising his fellow miners for their hard work and self sacrifice. Here are a few lines:

Ye can taalk aboot wor Air Force, wor Navy and wor Army, but folks whaat say that's aal wor strength, whey man, they're taalkin' barmy.

We're fightin' in the cause of Peace where ivvor wheels gan roond; where ivvor hearts beat willingly ti rhythmic hammer soond.

And ivvorytime a pitman says: 'By God, we'll see this through.'

It's one mair vital target-shot ti make a tyrant rue.

And ye can see the evidence of good owld British pluck where ivvor coals come flowin' doon to fill the waitin' truck.

Harry Speight writes of his time spent in the early war years at Ashington Colliery Brickworks (seen above): 'The machine house where I worked contained two machines which produced 12,000 bricks, per machine, every hour. Geordie White was in charge of the 'crusher'. That summer of 1940 was beautiful. The Battle of Britain was raging, and when the alarm sounded one sunny afternoon we all had to go to the shelter that was built under one of the shale heaps. The photo shows ARP men in full dress leaving a shelter in the pit yard during a practice air raid. There were at least one hundred men and boys in there, among them Jimmy Young's labouring gang. It was one of his gang, Jimmy Alexander, who kept our spirits high playing the top hits of the day on his mouthorgan.

'Sadly, I remember the day Geordie Brown, stripped to the waist, walked out of the brickyard kilns with his head bowed, speaking to no one. We found out later that he had just received news that his son, a pilot in the RAF, had been killed.'

This is a photo of ARP decontamination squad in July 1939. Seated: Andy Hay, J. Hughes, George Brown, D. Walker, Jim Alexander, J. Bookless, Fred Simm and George White standing far right. Dressers at back were J. Holland and J. Sample.

Two alien figures emerge from an Ashington Colliery shelter.

Pit Ponies at Royal Show, 1939
by Bob Thompson of Lynemouth Colliery

On the last day of the Show at Windsor, four of us were selected to sing 'Blaydon Races'. The Queen asked Fred Reavley of Linton Colliery if these were the clothes we wore down the pit. He said 'Yes'. Some of the ladies asked silly questions such as 'What were your reactions when coming to the surface after being underground for three years?'

R.N. Stephenson of Lynemouth Colliery said: 'During the day we were allowed some time off and we wore our pit clothes. Being probably the only pit lads they had ever seen, they stared at us so much that we were glad to put our ordinary clothes back on.'

J. Shaw of Ashington Colliery was asked: 'Are those pit ponies blind?' 'What do they cut their tails off for?' 'Do you carry the coals out of the pit on your back?'

Sep Sweet of Woodhorn Colliery said: 'I think the ponies must have eaten a stone of sugar every day because nine out of ten people fed them a sugar lump. I wish the Show had lasted six months.'

Victor Riches of Ashington Colliery said: 'Everyone we met was very sociable, but we met hosts of ill-informed people who now know a lot more about pit ponies and working conditions.'

Photo shows top left Bob Thompson with Turpin; top middle
Sep Sweet with Spot; top right Vic Riches with Noble. Bottom
left Edward Shaw with King; Fred Reavley with Jim; and
R. Stephenson with Geordie.

The miners were pleased when Sundays came around because, for some, that was the only full day when they didn't have to go to the pit. Miners had traditionally worked an eleven-day fortnight with only alternate Saturdays off; then the pits went on to a five-and-a-half day week. One favourite pastime was going for a family walk on a Sunday after tea. And what could be more peaceful than a stroll around the Hirst Flower Park, then to sit on a park bench and watch a game of bowls or simply appreciate the well-cultivated flowers and shrubs. Our photo is from the 1930s.

Seen here are a group of clerical workers at Ellington Colliery in 1945: Arthur Whinnom, William Graham cashier, Bob Rankin went into Time Office, Albert Smith, George Duncan, Jack Spowart went into Personnel, Robert Holmes, Verena Hall, Jean Crawford, Margaret Yole, Betty Potts, Rita Conway and Eunice Huntley.

Coal Industry Nationalised

At long last the mines were handed over to the workers on January 1st 1947. That day was acclaimed as being a great victory for the miners over the coalowners. In fact what happened was that the original colliery gaffers were kept on in their own jobs thus maintaining the status quo of the old ACC. This NCB leaflet was issued in advance of the big day.

Said Sir John Hall who was brought up in Railway Row, North Seaton: 'The men didn't have the managers to put in charge, so they couldn't take over. They sacked the Ashington Coal Company one day and gave them their jobs back the next. And what had it won the men? Absolutely nothing.'

Do you realise that on this man's work **depend all these** *The Nation's Treasure*

WE all know that coal is the basis of almost all British industry and transport, but we don't always carry this knowledge a step further and realise that our coal itself depends on the miner. That is why it is right that the coal miner should be one of the best paid industrial workers of the day.

There are plenty of miners in the North today and they are among the finest and most skilled in the world.

WHAT DO THEY EARN?

A boy of 14 who works underground earns up to 38/6 a week. **At 20** he will be earning up to 87/- a week and at **21** he cannot earn less than £5 a week underground (the guaranteed minimum wage), and in most cases, of course, he earns considerably more.

The North was in the forefront in the war and now the Northern miners are in the forefront of the industrial drive.

MEN OF THE NORTH FOR THE MINES OF THE NORTH

But Nationalisation was viewed as a moral victory, and on January 1st 1947, two female colliery clerks, Jean Cowan on left and Edna Henderson posed in the snow under a poster claiming that Ashington Colliery (and all the others) was now part of the National Coal Board. Jean, who became Mrs Miller, was the daughter of the Linton Colliery undermanager, and Edna, later to become Mrs Ralph, was for many years the headteacher's secretary at Ashington Grammar then High School.

For the time being at least, all was optimism in the pit-yards on New Year's Day 1947. A 30-second triumphal blast in the pit buzzer signalled the unfurling of the brand-new blue and white flag of the NCB at Ashington where the miners marched into the pit behind the Lynemouth Colliery Band.

This changeover had a marked effect on all parts of colliery work procedures, none more so than the locomotive department. On January 1st 1947 the North Northumberland Area (Ashington and the other four pits were in No 9 Area until 1950) took over 37 locomotives, the majority working on the Ashington system. A numbering scheme was introduced in 1955 (by then the Group of Collieries was in No 3 Area). When three diesels arrived in 1959 they were numbered in a new list beginning at 101. On March 26th 1967 this Area was combined with the South Northumberland Area to form a new Northumberland Area. This is a photo of No 10 loco with engine driver Fred Mather on far right and Harvey Smith first left. The other men were a gang of platelayers.

Ashington Colliery set up an 'Old Man's Set' which was a team of men who were over sixty years of age. This is how they were described in the *Ashington Post* in January 1949: 'Eight men of Ashington Colliery all over sixty and regarded by the management as "typical Northumbrian pitmen," set the pace as coal fillers for many of the younger generation at the colliery. As a team, these veterans have an average output of 408 tons with the absentee rate less than one per cent. The men work in a three-foot seam only a few minutes walk from the shaft bottom. The youngest of the team is 61 and the oldest is George Summers, aged 69. Mr J.T. Dodds, aged 63, of Bedlington, seldom misses a shift although he has to cycle from his home six miles away.' From left at back: George Nelson a union man, W. Dixon, M. Mills, W. Johnstone, T. Matthews, W. Main, George Summers, W. Heslop, Bobby Main union man at back right, and partly hidden J.T. Dodds.

'Hands like Shovels but Hearts of Gold'
by Dorothy Crowe (née Pattie)

I was born in Ashington into a mining family who lived in East Villas. After attending Hirst East Infants school, I went to Bedlington Grammar, leaving there to train to be a State Registered Nurse at Newcastle General Hospital between 1952-55. That's me on the photo, sitting just below Field Marshal Montgomery who had been persuaded to make the awards in 1955 by nursing tutor Cora Barron (sister of Normanton) who had been nurse with Monty in the desert during the Second Word War ...

When my son Jeff was old enough, I went back to work, destined to become a Ward Sister at Ashington Hospital. I worked on the Medical Wards, always very busy nursing the miners who had lost their health through pit-work, where Emphysema and Bronchitis had ruined their lives. I am pleased that some of them are now being compensated – nothing on earth could repay them for what they have suffered.

It was here that my mining education was improved as old cuttermen, wheezing like cuddies, taught me all about cutting coal. I loved these men; they were the salt of the earth, laughing when they had nothing to be cheerful about, and they were always nice to us nurses. They had hands like shovels but hearts of gold, and they worked themselves to death for their wives and bairns.

High Market Jnrs played their home games at the Rec in the late 1940s, as seen
in this photo. In 1947, Joe Grieve was a groundsman there and also the trainer
of these young lads. Joe later became secretary of the Joint Welfare Scheme.
From back left: Fred Hodgson, Tom Pigg, Bill Smith, Billy and Harry Neary,
Alan Bell, Joe Grieve. Front: Les Davison, Alan Houlison, Geordie Roy, Jim?
Hindmarsh, Brian Anderson and Ivor Dixon.

In 1948, Ashington FC were running a Junior team, hoping to bring
youngsters through into their first eleven. At this time George Cave was to the
fore in footballing circles. He is seen on the left with Frankie Clayton, Tom
Wear, John Waters, Ron Bennett, Tommy Liddle and Billy Edmondson. Front:
Les Renwick, Alan Young, Ernie Eastlake, Percy Armstrong and Ken Prior who
later came back to manage Ashington FC.

It was illegal to take photos down the pit after the Second World War, in case a spark from flashbulb ignited a pocket of gas. But miners had ways and means of recording their own images in a work situation. Here we have a set of fillers, either in the Bothal or Carl Pit around 1947. These lads are grouped in a main roadway about eight feet high, supported by steel arch girders. There are at least four of the Willis clan here, three of them at the back and Jimmy Willis, a concert chairman at the Comrades, seen third left at the front, next to him is Fen Shields and Bullock; the lad on right is Geordie who was a steward at the Fell 'em Doon Club; behind him is a chap who went into management at the Portland Hotel. Bob Ford is second left middle row.

Obviously taken the same day, these are four stoneman sitting next to the caunch (stone wall) in the mothergate. It was their job to blast down that wall of stone behind them so that the face conveyor could be moved forward. A safety lamp  hangs from the roof, its flame indicating that all was safe, as far as gas was concerned. Man on left, perched on the Blackett gear box of a scraper belt is a Lashley. On the right we have a Meco double XXL conveyor, with big John Hart far right. Other two unknown.

The game of Pitch and Toss was always a mystery except to the miners who played it. Here is how a conversation went at Ashington YMCA recently between a group of 'old timers'.

'Aye, whey, ye get a group o' men that gan tiv a place oot the road o' the polis. One man stands wiv two pennies on the forst two fingers of his hand. And he'll cry: "Heeds a half a dollar!" or whatever sartin amoont o' money he cares to name.

'Noo, in the big skeul, that was fivers and pund notes in them days. Noo, he has a man tekkin the money for him, and when he hoys them up'aheight, and if they land a heed and a tail – that's oneses – neebody wins – and the pennies hev ti gan back on his fingers. Noo, the man what picks them pennies up is a maraa of his, and he is caaled the 'bebber'. He cleans the pennies if they've been muckied, puts them back on the fingers and they are tails up-ower.

'He hoys them up again and if they come doon two heeds, he's won. They played doon by the Foxcover and had what the' caalled 'watchies' who would watch for the polis. And if he shooted: "Here's the polis comin'," everybody bolted. Cos the polis used to raid them regular. And there was another skeul at Old Tommy's cottage, down by the riverside.

'The Pitch and Toss was always even-money bets. There might be a group of up to fifty men, and one man might bet a tenner which somebody would cover, or there might be two separate five pund bets. If ye 'brock the skeul' that meant ye'd won the lot, and neebody had nowt left to keep ye gannin to bet again.

'The game began to wear oot because people were gettin' mair money, and there was different things to gammel on, like the dog-track. But in their day, they were very popular. Some lads used to finish the pit in foreshift on Friday mornin', gan straight doon to the skeul, and lose their week's pay. Aye, it was a great bit sport.'

The illustration is by YMCA stalwart, Bob Walkinshaw.

Another of the pitman's favourite pastimes was whippet racing. The miner was always fascinated by speed, whether it be Powderhall foot-runners or greyhounds. They couldn't own a greyhound at Portland Park in the early days so they took the next best thing – a whippet, not as fast but much more friendly. Whippet Sweeps took place in a variety of places such as Green Lane, North Seaton or here at the Hirst Welfare where Jim Nichol is seen letting the dogs out of the traps. On left is Russell Taylor, Alan Davison, Jim Nichol, Mike Hale, Tom Caldow and Pat Davison with pushchair. The three puppies racing were Toffee Crisp, The Toy and Mr Bud.

The unsung heroes of the Ashington Welfare Football League were its referees. For not much money, but a lot of verbal abuse, these men turned out in all weathers so that the young lads could get a game every  Saturday, sometimes in conditions that would have Premier League players reaching for their overcoats and snow shoes. Most of these lads were pitmen during the week, same as the players. Back, from the left: Jim Pattison and his son who became a crack golfer, Jim Wallace, Sammy Pringle a Priestman's Institute player, goalie was Ken Jordan, Billy Gibb, Bill Peary, Cyril Bird in the same school team as Jackie Milburn, Tom Rossiter with the flag. In front: Bob Dalkin, Joe Dalkin, Snowden Riddell and Les Dalkin who became a Football League referee, bottom right is Joe Gibbons. The game was against Hexham referees in 1948 and the team were entertained at night in the Queen's Hall, Hexham.

Another group who performed magnificently were members of the Salvation Army who did great work in the mining community, especially feeding the children of Ashington during the 1926 stoppage. The Salvation Army appeared in Ashington in 1889, using a church opposite the Seventh Row. However, there was also a Hirst Corps whose first entry in a log book was dated 27th September 1924. The Hirst Corps was based at a number of venues before buying the Methodist Church on Sycamore Street where they are seen on this early 1950s photo, back, from the left: W. Armstrong, A. Besford, E. Armstrong, J. Murdie, G. Forsyth, A. Clive, J. Baird, I. Murdie, G. Pattison, R. Smails, W. Pattison, K. Rogerson and S. Blears. Second back row: R. Murdie, J. Partland, T. Clark, D. Bennett, Humphrey, A. Hall, H. Armstrong, J. Wealleans, W. Kennedy. Second front row: W.J. Armstrong, T. McCullock, O. White, A. Partland, R. Armstrong, R. Humphrey, A. Howard, J.W. Lillico, L. White. Front row: F. Long, J. Archbold, G. Baird, F. Humphrey, W. Robinson, Adj Smith, Major Taylor, R. McCauley, J. Hooks, J. Ross, G.H. Elliott and W. Clark.

The Planning Department at Ashington Colliery had a 'grudge' cricket match at the Rec (probably against the Wages Department) in 1949. At stake was the 'Goesunder' Cup. From left: Ray Richell, John Johnson, Tony Wright, John Floyd, Jack Hays, Paul Clark, Jack Jones manager, Tim Brown, Albert Armstrong, Ted Shaw, Len Finlay, Eric Imrie, John Eke, Michael Mulligan, Gerry Thompson, Harry Boutland, Brian Woof, the small girl is Ann Finlay standing behind Jack Chrisp.

Hirst Athletic in 1949 had a great team of lads, mostly young pitman. Back: Gus Wilson, Ivan Wilson, Les Weddle, Gordon Richardson, Ray Logan. Front: Lol Weddle, Joe Smith, Ernie Charlton, Ron Talbot, Billy Edmondson and 'Sammy' Robinson.

This is a team of young lads who played for the Hirst Villa Juniors around 1949. The team was run by Louis Rogers who lived at Garden City Villas, as did some of the team. Most

of the lads worked underground or as mechanics. Back, from the left: Alan Duff, Jimmy Thompson, Colin Greenwood, Don Foster, Joe Bowden, Jackie Lawson, George McPherson, Alan White, Jimmy Carlton, Billy Cain, Alan 'Clankey' Longstaffe and Louis Rogers.

And here is a Hirst Villa senior squad in 1952 who beat the mighty East End in the quarter finals of the Booth Cup that year. Back: Harry Vout, Bob Tinkler, John Hale, Geordie Keys, John  'Butch' Birchall, Joe Parry, Bob Miller and Stan Branwell. Front: Pop Murdie, Sid McLean, Bob Lisle, John Jacques and Johnny Lisle.

Not pitmen, but pitmen's wives and daughters in this squad of Ashington Ladies who played at the Hirst Park in the early 1950s with Jackie Milburn as referee. Their goalkeeper was Brenda Brown with fullbacks Jean Ramm and Mary Purvis; midfield players were Jean Hollings, Sylvia Angus and Marina O'Keefe; with forwards Doreen Drape, Yvonne Rogers, Valerie Brown, Peggy Salkeld and Gwen Varty. Reserves present were Nancy Black, Marjorie Crawford, Ivy Blake and Minnie Crosby.

Talking of Jackie Milburn, this is Wor Jackie in 1951 shortly after scoring the two goals that beat Blackpool in the 1951 FA Cup Final, standing outside his house in Ellington Terrace with youngsters Jackie Swalwell and Ronnie Patterson. Said Ronnie: 'It was on a Sunday morning and I said to Jackie that we should go up to Jackie Milburn's house to get his autograph and have our photo taken with the great man. When we got there, his wife Laura made us most welcome and insisted that Jackie should pose with us.'

Some NCB Laboratory Girls from 1951. This hockey team photo was taken in the Dust Suppression Unit at Bothal Barns. Back row includes: Maureen Wilkinson, Olive Denwood, Audrey Conn, Elizabeth Drysdale, Marion McKillip. In front: Winnie Lyall, Angela Walkinshaw and Jean Porritt. Some other girls who worked in the Lab were: Brenda Davison, Pat Barrass, Sheila Hedley and Joan Smith.

Eleven mechanics drawn from local collieries were chosen to represent the NCB against teams of all-comers. The opponents this day in 1951 at Hirst Welfare were a team of miners from Scotland, in fact it was billed as a game of England v Scotland. Back row: Ron Dickenson, Ronnie Bennett, Bill Thompson, Fred Arthur, Cecil Leslie, Ronnie Raine and Jack Cook manager who went to USA. Front: Hughie 'Jock' Richmond trainer, George Nichol, Jim Young, Norman Campbell, Clifford Murdie, Jim Johnson and Mike McCall coach.

In 1951 a football match took place at Ashington Rec between the Fitters and the Apprentices. The young lads were in white. Back: Stan Sudlow, Bruce Mather, John Bacon, Lothar Muller, Sol Johnstone and Brian Morpeth. Front: Gordon Tulloch, Alan Weddell, John Scott, Norman Rollin and Peter Hankinson.

The Fitters were represented by, back: Ken Stephen, Joe Hall, Brian Anderson, Ray Hindhaugh, Ronnie Bennett and Clifford Murdie. Front: Jimmy Douglas, Malcolm Taylor, Bob Cookson, Alan Atkinson and Straughan Richardson.

It is unusual to get an all-action photograph, but this shows the two above teams with the Fitters pressing hard on the Apprentices' goal. Note the colliery buildings in background. The goalkeeper seen, young Lothar Muller, sadly died of leukaemia at nineteen years of age, shortly after this game.

Hirst East End in 1953 were represented with this squad. Back: Ken Steven, Tot Burns, Bill Southern, Gus Wilson, Tom Liddell, Walter Harmison. Front: Bill Mearyweather, Percy Armstrong, Pop Anderson, Jimmy Milburn and Ron Talbot. The late Walter Harmison's sons and grandsons continue to make their mark on the local sporting scene.

Priestman's Institute on North Seaton Road, more famous for turning out billiard and snooker players, started to run a football team in the Ashington Welfare League in the late 1950s. This is the squad in 1959  with a brand-new set of strips bought from Frank Brennan's sports shop on North Seaton Road. Back: Michael Kirkup, John Mather, Brian Robinson, John Barker, Tom Herron, Bob Mavin and trainer Norman Johnson. Front: Jackie Parmley, Keith Johnson, Derek King, Derek Parmley and Parry. The photo was taken, as were so many teams in the '50s and '60s, by Jack Laws.

Pit trainees were given a blue boiler-suit and 16 weeks of intensive training at Ashington. Some of the staff were Jack Kirkup, Tom Patterson, Cud Pringle and Jack Crook, with Mr Charlton as manager and Joe Dockerty as Safety Officer. These 1951 lads are back, left to right: Ron Thompson, Joe Cain, Sid Smith, Derek Chesney, Les Atkinson, Alan Brotherton, Jim Potts, Eric Thompson, Tom Dawson, Alan White, Mr Charlton, unknown, unknown. Front: unknown, unknown, Jackie Lothian, Charlie Mann, Fenwick Cook, unknown, Brian Lowes and Bruce Mather.

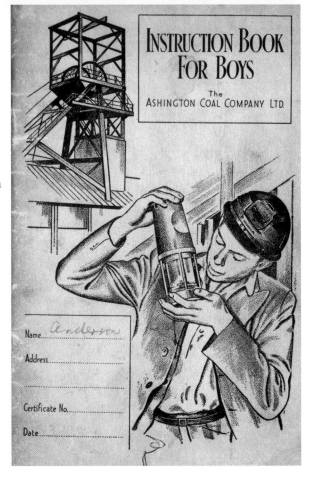

INSTRUCTION BOOK FOR BOYS

The ASHINGTON COAL COMPANY LTD.

Name............ Anderson

Address............

....

Certificate No............

Date............

The young trainees from 1942 onwards were given a training manual that highlighted the dangers that might be encountered while underground.

This photo is headlined 'In the Cage' with the advice: 'A bar is provided overhead in the cage, hold it like the lads in the picture. Before getting into the cage search your pockets for cigarettes and matches.'

Hanging Front Clip on to Haulage Rope. 'Stand at the side of the tub and place the clip on the rope close to the tub. Before hanging your clip on see that the track in front is clear.'

Taking Clips Off. 'You should attempt to take the clip off immediately the last tub has got on to the landing. As in the photo, a bat sometimes needs to be used to slacken off tight clips.'

Controlling Tubs with Iron Drags. 'Hold your drags firmly with the loop in the vertical position. This will prevent the loop and your fingers being jammed. A front-wheel drag will stop tubs sooner than a back-wheel drag. Look after your drags – you need them.'

Editor: In sharp contrast, here we see a young lad riding the limbers, probably in the 1920s. He is not following any of the rules laid down in our 1942 manual. Someone has scrawled in chalk on a wooden chock what looks like 'George W. Laws' – perhaps this young lad's name? That bedraggled pony was once pure white – see how the grime of the mine is ingrained into its coat.

Derailments. 'If when driving or putting your tub gets off the way, loose your pony from the tub, to lift it back on.'

Coal Putting through Canvas Doors. 'When riding the limbers and passing through canvas sheets, lean close up to the pony with your head forward, and raise your arm to ward the sheet of your head.'

This is a group of pit fitters and apprentices in 1954. Back: Jimmy Wilson, Fred Arthur, Bruce Mather, Alan Weddell, Joe Hall and Ray Hinhaugh. Front: Alan Atkinson, Percy Armstrong, Alec Todd Jnr, Geordie Drinkwater and Ernie Dobbinson.

And this is a group of trainees in 1950. What makes this photo stand out from the crowd is the presence of big Jack Charlton, even then at fifteen years of age, towering over his mates, bare-headed, back row centre. The pit instructor standing in front of Jack is one Jack Kirkup MBE. Big Jack only lasted about six months at the pit – he spent a lot of that time on the spirals at Linton Colliery where his father worked. Jack was spotted playing football at the Hirst Park by a Leeds United scout – the rest, as they say, is history.

And history was surely made in August 1966 when the two Charlton boys, Jack and Bobby, were feted by their home town of Ashington for being the first pair of brothers to have played for a World Cup-winning team when England beat Germany that year. This photo was  taken on Station Bridge shortly before the pair got out of the car to go into the council chambers where they each received a gold watch for their achievement. Crowds of youngsters, clutching autograph books, had waited hours in the colliery row of Beatrice Street for the illustrious brothers to make an appearance in the white Rolls Royce, specially loaned for the occasion.

Diary Dates at Woodhorn Colliery
by George Tully

1941, December 20th – Woodhorn Fan House and Crab Engine House were hit by a bomb.

1942, January 17th – new Steam Fan driven by electric motor started at Woodhorn Colliery.

1944, April 3rd – Maurice Abbott started as undermanager.

1951, January 9th – Billy Aisbett retired from pit.

1952, February 4th – Nicky Chapman died down Woodhorn Pit on the 'T' middle bord.

1952, September 11th – Bob Wilkinson's leg was broken in 7th Dip.

1953, April 13th – new Medical Centre opened at Woodhorn with Sister Pearson in charge.

1959, April 22nd – the NEEB switched current on to Woodhorn New Power Station.

1959, October 5th – Sid Lumb started as assistant electrical engineer at Woodhorn.

1959, September 2nd – Tot Smith Woodhorn Colliery Manager was hurt.

1960, September 9th – all local pits started their third week's holiday.

1960, September 26th – the 100 hp trunk belt was installed in Woodhorn's No 1 Staple.

Woodhorn Colliery in the 1960s.

One date for the diary at Ashington Colliery was January 30th 1950 at precisely 11.30 am. That was when this curious accident occurred in Ashington pit-yard. Ken Lillico explains: 'Tankeys used to freewheel along the back of Bridge House and could not be seen or heard. That day, the cobbled area of the road adjacent to the

footbridge steps was covered with ice; the sudden appearance of the tankey took the crossing-keeper and the driver of the van by surprise. The van driver could not stop on the icy cobbles so the van was squeezed between the engine and the fence-post. Amazingly, neither of the two occupants in the van was seriously injured.'

In the foreground, holding the flag was the gateman Bill Dixon; wearing glasses was the loco shed foreman, Tom Richardson; the small man at front could be a fitter called Tom Bland; Tommy Temple of Rail Control was probably in this group together with Colliery Polis, Joe Smith. One of the tankey drivers was Freddie Priest, but the driver of loco No 13 that day was Bobby Lawrence.

The NCB Planning Department in 1952, according to Edwin Grieve: 'Played all sorts of games, especially against the lasses from the NCB Offices; we played Polo at Ashington Swimming Baths, and Netball in the garage that belonged to the United bus company – the lasses got ready in one bus and us lads in the other – one

day there was a right squeal when it was discovered that Mick Mulligan had hidden himself in the rack of the lasses' bus. Some of the lads on this cricket team came to us as 'Directed Practical Trainees' and lodged at the White Elephant. Back: John Mitchison, Mick Mulligan, John Scott, John Bell, Cliff Warne, Roddy McKechnie. In front: Grant Stobbart, Tim Brown, Edwin Grieve, Brian Woof and Stan Slatcher of Derbyshire.'

Head horsekeeper at Woodhorn, Charlie Wilkinson (seen on left) lived in No 8 Woodhorn Colliery, one of the gaffer's houses. In 1952 he took Woodhorn's favourite pony, the black and white Royal, to Newton Abbot for the aptly named Royal Show where he was presented to the newly-crowned Queen Elizabeth II. Charlie had emigrated to Australia in 1926 because of the depression, but returned two years later where he was set on at Woodhorn Pit. When Charlie retired in 1963 there were still about 80 ponies stabled underground at Woodhorn.

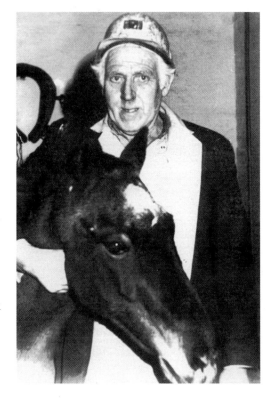

Geordie Phillips has the distinction of being the last horsekeeper at Woodhorn Colliery when it closed in 1981. Geordie said: 'I began as a putter at Woodhorn in 1938. After a spell on filling I developed a beat knee so I was set on as assistant horsekeeper in the Yard Seam stables where they had 125 ponies, and there were 80 in the Low Main as well. This photo, taken by Jack Wallace, is of me and 'King'. When the pit was set to close they brought all the ponies out and sent them to Ellington, but four were kept on bank in the surface stables – Rod, King, Brig and Smokey. They were taken down the pit each day by the salvage workers. They were there till June 1981, and when they finished, so did I.'

Robert Gilholme was horsekeeper at Lynemouth Colliery from 1948 to 1964 during which time he took pit ponies to various Royal Shows, including Windsor. The photo shows Bob with pony, 'Roy' from Lynemouth Pit who had won the Cup for Best Pony that year and had also been successful in the Ashington Show.

The time was 6 am, the place Ashington Railway Station, and the year was early 1950s. The reason this large group of mostly local miners was gathered here was to catch a train to Tranmere to support Ashington FC in the First Round proper of the FA Cup. Some of the faces belong to, from left on ground, Bob Dodds a deputy who lived at Stakeford, Stan Agan, Bobby Algar with banjo, curly Jack Thompson, a couple of unknowns then George Tait. Far left standing with apple in hand is little Jackie Lawson, 6th in is Adie Brown, then father and son John Robert Stewart (in trilby with white band) and his son John; two lads in centre are Tom Crosby and Tom McPherson; big man is Albert Fowler, smiling face with receding hairline belongs to Walter Potts, and man with pipe is Tom Lyall former manger of the Meadow Dairy and owner of a shop in Castle Terrace. Towards the rear of the group is George Redpath and you can just spot the top half of Jack Hamilton's trilby back right.

It was party time for these NCB officials and their partners in December, 1953. This event was held at the Arcade Dancehall, which has rarely seen so much glam and glitter – and that was just the men! There were more pit gaffers at this 'do' than you could swing a pick at. Back: Miss Joan Riches, Mr & Mrs Jack Hay, Len Finlay, Charles Bewick, Edna Ralph, Donald Hindson, Bill Riches, Tim Brown, Paul Clarke, Lorna Makepeace and Dick Miles who later married. Front: Betty Triplow, Brenda Davison, then Mesdames Bewick, Hindson and Riches.

And at yet another NCB Ball in 1956, we see a young surveyor, John Hall, and his good lady at the Rex Hotel, sipping Mateus Rose, at their annual shindig. Sir John said later: 'We used to go to the Rex on a hired bus, and thought we were all so grand, sitting in this posh Rex Hotel, drinking our *Mateus Rose* – I wouldn't be caught dead drinking that rubbish now.'

Sir John's surveying colleagues present were, back row: Bob Dickinson, Roy Tateson, unknown and Raymond Poxton. Seated: Norah Dickinson, Elsie Sharp, Mrs Redpath, Mae (Lady Mae) Hall, John Hall, Jim Sharp, Ernie Rowe and Brenda Poxton.

Editor: I began working at Duke Street Coal Depot in 1959 when there were only three men there, and I was to take over from Herbie Owen who was to be transferred to Lynemouth. But as coal production went up and up, there were soon six people working in a square box that should have only had three. Tommy Tinkler came from Woodhorn, Terry Saunders, back from his jaunt in Australia, moved in; John Forster became a fixture; Geordie Cowell was employed; Percy Whitlelaw was transferred from Ellington Depot; Geordie Charlton moved from his job as second-man on the wagons to come inside; various men who had been hurt down the pit were given a temporary job till they recuperated – that included Cecil Wood, Jimmy Slaughter and Stu Sinclair; Eric Imrie, involved in an horrific train accident also worked there for a period, as did many others.

The photo shows a group from Duke Street enjoying a night out at the Linton & Woodhorn Club in 1962. From left: George Cowell, Geordie Nichol, John Forster, Stu Sinclair, Billy Mason, Mike Kirkup, Tommy Tinkler and Geordie Charlton.

This photo is of a Safety Awards presentation to colliery drivers outside the Wages Office at Ashington Colliery in 1949. Perhaps only a couple of these men are still alive, such as Malcolm Smith, fifth left middle row, and Jim Maxwell second left front row. Tommy Tinkler is third left middle row, and a grand old-timer Forster Proudlock is second right middle row.

Jackie Milburn was very friendly with one of the NCB drivers, Malcolm Smith, who persuaded Jackie to let the other lorry drivers have their photos taken wearing Jackie's international caps. Jackie seems to have amassed nine up till this date, probably around 1951, but he went on to win thirteen caps in all. Jackie on the right is talking to Arthur Taylor.

With the advent of the motor lorry to deliver workmen's coal, another breed of men took to the streets – they were the hoyers in of coal. And reigning supreme was Jack Harris, alias Jack the Coalman. If one or two housewives thought they might get the better of Jack and not pay him his dues, then Jack hoyed the coals back out of the cree. It seems incredible that Ashington which owed its very existence to coal is now registered as a 'smokeless zone'. That would have brought tears to Jack the Coalman's eyes.

Being a Coalmerchant
by Eric Nichol

One of the first things you have to do to be a coalman is to find a shovel – that is the most important part of the job – find a 'shull'. You didn't buy a new one, that would be a dead giveaway that you were the new boy and ideal bait for others taking the mickey. No, you looked around for a worn one, and believe me there were plenty.

Grandad Nichol started the coal business in Ashington before I was even thought of; and my father and uncle just carried on after the first war, so there were plenty of worn shovels to choose from. My hands trembled with the thoughts of grasping this magnificent piece of equipment that was the shull, but little did I realise that this shull would soon have my tiny hands full of calluses.

There were plenty of characters in the trade, none more so than the man who worked for George Beattie – one George Nichol (no relation). But what a grand fellow he was, nothing was too much for him. He was the sort of person who, even today, you would not hesitate to contact if you needed help. Not only did he have an ear for your trouble, he had a sense of humour that was hard to equal.

This has been a description of my introduction to being a coalman. But if it were not for the coal being dug from the ground by brave men I could not have written it.

Margaret Brannigan, daughter of Jimmy Little, first manager at Duke Street Depot, remembers when she worked in Ashington Colliery Wages Department.

'It was lovely to work there because everyone knew each other. The worst day was when we had to fill up the small containers with cash. Each had a number on the bottom, and you had to sort them out by number and place them on these big racks. You had to check what each man's tally was, then see how much he had to draw before getting filthy, stuffing pound notes in the bottom of the tin, then filling it up with loose coins. We were paying a lot of money out in the 1950s. It was funny to see men scratching around for stubs from checks with perhaps ten shillings less than they had to draw – that was their 'keepy-backs'.'

When the Wages department had their annual Christmas Party at the Newcastle House (now Waterford Lodge) in Morpeth in 1956, those present were, back row: Elsie Proctor, Andy Rankin, Ted Shaw, Dennis Doyle, Sandie Crombie, Bill?, Muriel Charlton, unknown and Jim Davison. Second back row: Margaret Smailes, Marjorie Patterson, Ruby Fotheringham, Len Finlay, Marjorie Denton, Vera Reed, Ivy Hindmarsh, Edna Gair, Elizabeth Walker, Alan Sweet and Bob Hay. Second front row: Albert Armstrong, Ann Tapson, John Miller, Judy Ingle and Mary Hornsby. Front: Sam Coxon, Flo Storey, Michael?, Margaret Little and Fred Weddell.

A group of Woodhorn fitters in 1958. Included in the back row: Bob Kirk, Brian Wren, Ron Mitcheson and Alan Taylor. Front row: Bill Whitcombe, Jack Gillis and Jim Thompson; centre right with glasses Jim Macfarlane.

'Linton Colliery was closed down with barely a whimper from anyone.' So says Colin Moody who contrived to be the last man out of Linton Pit – not a bad record considering that it was his grandfather who helped to sink the shaft way back in the 1890s. This photo shows the men

from the Joiners' and Wagon Shops in 1961 who were later transferred to Ashington Workshops when Linton closed in 1968. Back men with no heads: Tommy Walker and Bob Railston. Back row: unknown, an Ashington worker, unknown, Jimmy Harrison, Roy Henderson, Harry Railston, Clare Thompson, Henna Robson, Josh Gray, Russell Swan and Norman Scott. Front: Tommy Mackie, Colin Moody and Harry Jones.

Linton Youth Club decided to send a group of their members down the pit in 1954. From left: Bob English a deputy, Edith Curry (née Ramsden), Ann Dawson (née English), Joan Moody (née Dixon), Sheila Shields (née English), Andy Dixon master shifter, Ronnie Owens, Margaret Straughan (née Embleton), George Straughan, Jackie Dodds and Joyce Bractie (née Little).

The Linton squad in this photo were 1957-58 joint champions of the Northumberland Miners' Welfare League. Back: Les Robson, Jackie Dodds, Grant Stobbart, Colin Moody, Les Weddell and Watty Thornton. Front: Tommy Matthews, George Down, Innes Appleby, Colin Cairns and Jimmy Chirnside.

Football Fame came to Linton when they were featured in the May 1961 edition of *Coal News*. It reported: 'Of 153 dwelling houses in Linton, 149 are miners' homes. During the last forty years, men from the village have spread the football fame of Linton far and wide: Jim Kelly, captain of First Division Blackpool; NFA coach Tommy Rigg who followed his goalkeeping days with Watford and Gillingham with a spell as Gateshead's trainer; Bobby Yorke went on to play for Bradford City and Blyth; Les Dalkin, a member of the 1930s Linton Juniors, is today (1961) a top-ranked Football League referee.' And so it went on. Another fine footballer to come out of Linton was Josh Gray whose playing career was cut short by a horrible accident.

And these were some of the last miners to go down in the cage at Linton Pit in September 1968. Included are: Joe Price, Alan Messenger, Peter Minoughan, Ted Thompson, Ed Robinson, Alan Bowden, Bob Burns, Tom Douglas, Gordon Thompson and Geordie Gibson.

Ashington Colliery Stores, Supplies, Kalamazoo and Typing Departments, 1953. Margaret Curran (née Turnbull) says: 'We are standing outside the wooden hut where we worked – it was next to the Joiners' Shop where my father Jack Turnbull worked. I worked in the Stores from being

sixteen in 1953 up to when I was married in 1959. My husband is Jim Curran who worked at Ellington Colliery. Back left of photo is Margaret Miles, then Brenda McLawrence, Mary?, June Hirst, Lillian Lyons, Vivien Nesbitt. Second row: Sylvia Charlton, Lillian Short, Margaret Turnbull (me) and Eunice Tait. In front is Audrey Ferguson.'

NCB Area Workshop girls in 1959. Sheelagh Evans (née Gordon) says: 'We were the first staff at the Ashington NCB Workshops. From left is Marjorie Brown, then Evelyn Whitfield, Sheelagh Evans and Joyce Sweet. Maurice Anderson and I were transferred

from the Wages Department and the other girls were new to the coal industry. The trouble was that they moved us before the Workshops were built so we had to work in a Nissen hut in the middle of the pit yard. It was so dirty that if a piece of paper was left on the desk at lunchtime it was covered in soot in an hour. The Workshop manager then was Mr Smith with A. Tennick as deputy. After a year we were moved again to Linton, to converted pit-head baths.'

Area Planning Department group in the early 1960s. Said Marjorie Williams: 'I worked there from 1959 to 1974 as a Tracer, and I also worked in the Survey offices at Ellington and Pegswood. While updating plans at Swarland House, Amble, I met my now husband John Williams who left the NCB to qualify as a Civil Engineer. On photo back left is Jack Finlay, then Ned Anderson, Jack Summers, John Mitchison, Roddy McKechnie, Joe Armstrong, John Scott, George Bolton, Dave Gibson and Audrey Conn. Second row: May Parkinson, Grant Stobbart, Brian Woof, John Jamieson. Front row: Tim Bown, Jim Robinson and Dennis Holmes.

It was fitting that Jackie Milburn's 'third' statue, and arguably the best, should hold pride of place during the summer of 1996. Tom Maley's sculpture was eventually taken to St James' Park where it stood for over a year in the concourse leading to the ground. Sadly, Newcastle United could not come up with the necessary funds to have the statue done in bronze as Mr Maley would have wished. Jackie Milburn worked for about six months at Woodhorn, in fact, the men were going to go on strike at one stage because the pit manager refused to let Jackie have time off to travel to United's away games. The manager relented.

Some of the footballers playing in the 1950s are featured on this photo taken by Mike Parker at Woodhorn Colliery Museum, posing in front of Jackie Milburn's statue. The event, staged in 1996, was called: 'Ashington's Football Heroes', and many of these lads, by now in their sixties and seventies, played like heroes for local teams and also as professionals. From left: Ronnie Harrison, Louis Rogers, unknown, Alan White, unknown, Cyril Beddard, Percy Armstrong, 'Sam' Robinson, Josh Gray, Jimmy Hill, George Down, Joe Jones, Malcolm Smith, Raymond Poxon, Ken Steven, Mike Kirkup, Ron Coulson, Harry Harle, Jim Slaughter, Jack Leslie, Harry Speight and Bill Southern.

That same event brought together three of the best pro runners in the area. Footrunning, as it was called, was in its heyday just after the Second World War. Hundreds of local lads bought themselves a pair of running pumps and became sprinters every Saturday afternoon throughout the summer months. Each colliery village staged a foot handicap to coincide with the local Flower Show, and dozens of bookies lined the makeshift tracks, usually laid out on a football field, so that a popular distance was a mere 80-yard dash. Prizes varied between twenty and one hundred pounds, depending on the locality. But to win the coveted gold medal at Scotland's Powderhall meeting on New Year's Day was every pitman's ambition. And these three men did exactly that: Edwin Poxton on left, George 'Dusty' Down, and Harry Harle, all flashed past the post in first place and became pro-running legends.

This is the last pit pony to come out of the Carl Pit at 1.20 pm December 23rd 1969. The handler here is Bill Weddell, head horsekeeper. The banksman who brought this lucky beast to the surface was Harry Freeman.

Ashington Colliery 'Dosco' Record Breakers. Taken by Jack Wallace in the early 1970s, we see the men responsible for breaking the record for advancing an underground roadway using a Dosco machine. Back row: Jim Hagelburg, Doug Morris, George Rogerson fitter, Ken Kaye production manager, Fred Armstrong, John Knox undermanager, Jack Rollin. Middle row: John Wake, Mick Drysdale, Clive Robinson electrician, Jim Patrick, Joe Dobbinson overman, Pop Anderson, Taffy Longstaffe, Jim Hall deputy, Bob Carr, Dennis Cribbes, then a student. Front row: Eddie Thain, unknown, Lance Burton, Larry Lavelle personnel manager, Allan Spratt deputy manager, Ian McGregor, Percy Armstrong engineer, Jim Moffat electrician, and Ken Slaughter overman.

PIT CLOSURES
IMMINENT

Linton Colliery, Ashington

Rationalisation was the buzz word of the early 1970s. Linton Colliery, above, had already closed in September 1968. George Hetherington was manager of Ashington Colliery in 1973 with Herbie Swinburne and J. Knox as his undermanagers. The number of miners at Ashington Pit then was 1,062 while there were only 210 men working on bank. It was quite a drop from the heady days when that pit was at its peak just after the Second World War. Linton Colliery (above) had closed in 1968, and only 655 men in total worked at Woodhorn Colliery, managed then by C. Fenwick with C. Kenny and J. Errington. At Ellington, with a management team of Tot Smith, A. Spratt, G.W. Allison, Tot Burns and R. Ashurst, miners underground totalled 1,329 with 160 on the surface. Lynemouth in 1973 was still seen as the area's biggest employer with over 1,800 men in total working at the colliery under a team consisting of manager M. Widdas, Jack Tubby and Ernie Dundbar, with undermanagers S. Burke, R. Lillico, A. Potts, A.C. Cessford, and A. Baggaley. (Figures from *Colliery Guardian*.)

Photo shows miners' union officials on February 26th 1972 congregating at Ashington Institute prior to marching through the town. These men were mainly from the Mechanics' Union, such as Jack Thompson and Bob Wallace, while Ron Cummings and Jim Locker, members of the Ashington Colliery Band, are on right.

Here, the parade is about to reach the Grand Corner. The first men in the march were from Ashington Colliery, then Ellington and Lynemouth and, bringing up the rear were miners from Woodhorn who had not even left the Harmonic Hall when this photo was taken. Centre of the front line is George Grant then the local MP.

A meeting of the 1972 Strike Committee was held in the Premier Club. Some of the men were front, from the right: Bill Clyde a well-known leek grower, Ed Straker one time Woodhorn Canteen manager, Alec Wallace, big Jock Marshall, Chambers, big John Hart, John Murphy, Percy Drew, little Sammy Scott, Jim Freathy and unknown. Towards the centre of middle row is the late Denis Murphy between John Evans who lived in Woodhorn Road, and Cecil Wood.

In November 1976, miners' union leader Joe Gormley paid a whistle-stop visit to Ellington Colliery on his way to Woodhorn, Ashington and Lynemouth. He was there to campaign for support for early retirement. But the NCB were insisting it could only be for men at 64 years of age or those with 25 years' service. Note the board that says 'refrain from using obscene language'. That was a laugh for Sammy Scott and the other pitmen.

By the time we come to the penultimate chapter of coalmining in 1984, only Ashington and Ellington Collieries remained. Woodhorn had ceased to draw coal in 1981 and Lynemouth had been merged with Ellington to form a Combine, ceasing to be a coal-producer in 1983. The then Tory leader, Margaret Thatcher, pursued a head-on confrontation with miners' leader Arthur Scargill – an irresistible force against an immovable object. As the song says 'Something's gotta give'. A bitter strike began.

In November 1984, a young cub reporter for the *Morpeth Courier* was told to cover the story of a confrontation of police and striking miners at Ashington Central Workshops. Her name was Linda Stevenson. This is what her ex-miner husband Neil had to say: 'Because of the animosity towards the Press, Linda was a bit apprehensive about the whole thing, and asked me if I would go with her on the 'shoot'. This I did and, apart from some verbal unpleasantness from the more loud-mouthed of the strikers, we were able to come away unscathed.'

In the February 1985 edition of the *Northumbrian Miner*, under a heading of 'A Colliery Mechanic's Viewpoint', this is what a young Denis Murphy, now our Member of Parliament, then President of the Northumberland Colliery Mechanics' Association, had to say: 'In order to appreciate the current dispute we need to go back to the beginning of March 1984 and the NCB's proposals to the NUM when the North East Area NCB Director had said that if Lynemouth Colliery was closed, the finances of Northumberland would be balanced and no closures or cut-backs were being considered in the future. That promise, like many others in the past, has proved worthless. In March 1984, the NCB proposed:

1. Bates Colliery should reduce its manpower to approximately 600 men.

2. Ashington Coal Preparation Plant and the internal railways should close along with its coal stocking at New Moor and its Duke Street Depot.

3. Coal to be transported by road from Ashington and Brenkley to Lynemouth. The new stocking site would be at Lynemouth requiring the removal of surface buildings, resulting in the loss of 300 jobs.

'The North East Area of the NCB produced a secret document in October 1984 which indicated the demise of the Northumberland Coalfield within ten years … these are facts, not scaremongering.'

The late Denis Murphy, then President of the Northumberland NUM, had this to say in the same 1985 magazine:

'The situation as I see it is very simple: Northumberland has five pits, plus Lynemouth which acts as a satellite for Ellington, employing 5,500 of my members plus those of other affiliated unions ... I see my job as being to maximise the job potential of the British coal industry ... Let us make no mistake about it – it was an inflammatory act to appoint Mr Ian McGregor as Chairman of the NCB. He took on a mandate for this (Tory) government, and if we had allowed him to carry it out he would have crucified the Coal Industry similarly to that of Steel ... I do not wish to prolong this dispute one day longer than necessary. I do not wish to continue the hardship experienced by my members and their families ... The NUM are perfectly willing to negotiate at any time but without pre-conditions.'

A month before the strike began there was a bad omen. In February 1984, Desmond Sharp, a thirty-five year old father of two, had been killed when hit by a single large stone at Ashington Colliery where he was employed as a power loader. His death was to have dreadful repercussions on his wife and family.

Denis Murphy, former President of Northumberland Mechanics' Association now local MP.

Denis Murphy, then President of Northumberland NUM.

Anatomy of a Strike

adapted from a dossier compiled by Bill Harris, Miners' Compensation Secretary

The Lead-up

In 1981 a new redundancy scheme was introduced by the NCB. Men over fifty could get a lump sum payment, a weekly wage based on the equivalent of the 'dole', and a coal allocation. It was too good an offer to refuse, and hundreds of local miners took their redundancy. By 1984 the average age of a miner in the Ashington area was thirty-five.

By then Woodhorn Colliery had closed in March 1981 and Lynemouth Colliery ceased coal production in November 1983. Ellington Colliery (the Super Pit) employed 1,800 men – it was the only big production pit left in the area, although Ashington Colliery was still producing coal on a small scale.

Young miners with small families and big mortgages looked to Ellington Colliery for their futures. It also became the intake pit for men from other pits after theirs had closed.

In the autumn of 1983, Ian McGregor, then aged seventy-two, was appointed chairman of the National Coal Board by Margaret Thatcher. His brief was to close pits. He visited Ellington Colliery on February 22nd 1984, where he fell to the ground following a disturbance by miners. It was a bad start for the forthcoming strike.

March 12th 1984: A nationwide strike begins against the NCB's pay offer of 5.2%. This marked the beginning of pit closures. The miners of Scotland, Yorkshire and Wales came out on unofficial strike.

March 13th: Violence flares as pit strikes split miners. Only 21 of Britain's 174 mines are still working normally. The strikes that began in Scotland and Yorkshire are now official. Collieries in Nottingham, the county's second largest coalfield, have become the focus of attention. Militant strikers travel to Nottingham to picket the working pits. A 'flying picket' from Yorkshire dies outside Ollerton Colliery. His death intensifies dispute. Ashington is like a battle-zone with mass pickets coming in from outside collieries in Durham and Whittle. There were long lines of policemen and so-called battle-buses carrying frightened strike-breakers.

March 14th: A big Rally at North Seaton Welfare Institute confirmed that Ashington, Ellington and Lynemouth Collieries were picketed out. Northumberland flying pickets were organised at this meeting. Here we see a small group outside the Trade Union Hall. Jimmy Johnson, a Scot, in centre, was a volunteer driver on flying picket duty; the two others are Marie and Les Smith.

Miners from their own collieries were take to their pit gates as pickets, otherwise there might have been trouble from outside pickets. Local members accepted this agreement. The man sitting alone on picket duty is Bob Sawyer.

A mass demonstration against police violence was held in Ashington starting from NUM headquarters in Lintonville Terrace. A march led by Union officials paraded along Station Road to outside the police station where a sit-in took place as on our photo, also one on Station Road and at the Grand Corner.

Editor: My father Jack Kirkup was to be buried that same day on April 3rd 1984. He had died a few days earlier at the age of eighty-two. The service was to be held at St Aidan's RC Church in Park Road, Ashington. I vividly remember that, as the mourners were coming out of the church, we were met with the sight of hundreds of men marching behind their pit banners. To a man, as a sign of respect, the march halted and moved to the side of the road to enable the funeral cortege to leave the church and a policeman removed his helmet. The cortege moved back down Park Road, so missing the striking miners performing a 'sit-down' outside the Police Station. The out-of-work miners are seen here in the same photo as workmen, disregarding the demonstration, being too busy digging up the pavement outside what had originally been the Harmonic Hall, built so that miners could enjoy making music.

Woodhorn had closed in February 1981, but there still had to be a degree of maintenance to the shaft and also the roadways that provided ventilation for the Ashington miners. Four men plus a deputy were delegated to travel underground from Ashington every day to provide safety and security at Woodhorn. One of the last deputies to go there was Derek Longstaffe. Three of the miners who were regulars to go to Woodhorn were Harry Clyde, Josh Yearham and Brian Auld (his father Joe was the man killed in 1963).

Said Brian: 'That was the best job I ever had in my life! Pit manager, George Hetherington, had told us that we would still be paid underground wages even though much of our time was spent on bank.

'This is a photo outside the engineer's office next to No 1 Winding House. I am on the left with Josh Yearham; the two other men were a deputy and a pumper. The young lad was Josh's son Mark with Jess the dog.'

'We did this for five years between 1981-1986. One of the highlights of this time was when a camera crew arrived and began to shoot a film called 'The Captain's Tale' which was the story of how West Auckland won the first World Cup. I was given a small part in the film as a banksman, the man who let the main actors into the cage. In effect they only went about twenty yards down the shaft. A mock-up coal face was built in one of the offices on bank. Two of the actors were Tim Healey and Richard Griffiths, but the captain of the team was Dennis Waterman whose photo is on front cover of book. And this is a photo of me, on right, with a few extras in 1910 period costume and hairstyle, waiting outside the Woodhorn Baths building.

'After the year-long strike of 1984-85 I was proud to be amongst those who received a badge and a certificate for not giving in and for not being a scab. However, after a short time back at work I was badly hurt while the Woodhorn Museum was being put into effect. I was walking across a concrete slab that broke in the middle, pitching me six feet to the ground. I suffered a fractured back, and had to give up work through deteriorating and ill health.'

June 7th: Over 120 miners are arrested in London as fighting breaks out near Westminster during a mass rally when the Ashington banner hit the headlines in Fleet Street.

June 15th: A miner picketing outside a Yorkshire power station is killed.

September 9th: Ian McGregor, complete with paper bag over his head, arrives at Edinburgh for talks with miners' leader, Arthur Scargill.

October 10th: Having ruled that the miners' strike was unlawful, the High Court fined the NUM £200,000 and Arthur Scargill £1,000 for contempt of court.

October 24th: The deputies' union, NACODS, calls off its threatened strike.

Although the community spirit in the region was good for the first few months, the deputies' decision *not* to support the Strike in October 1984 was a big set-back. Everyone knew that if the deputies came out then the pits would soon be flooded; gas in the mines could have exploded, and the pits would have closed themselves. This was the last straw for many local miners, fed up with  months of deprivation. Strike-breaking came to the Ashington district for the first time. A favourite pastime was the guessing game: 'Who will be the first man to break the Strike?' There were few surprises when the crunch came. Here we see the Lynemouth Colliery 1984-85 strike committee. From back left: Gerald Clark, Peter Moran, Stevie Lawson, Bob Sawyer, Ronnie Martin and Mack Hedley. Front: John Dunn, Alan Lavelle, Andy Howard and Bill Harris.

The gloom and despair of the pit strikes of the 1920s fell over the area again. The only difference being that then there was no strike-breaking. Now scabs' families were split asunder by friends and relations going through picket lines. Scabs hid in their homes rather than face the wrath of the pickets. But there were still ugly scenes in social clubs and public places. The blacklegs may have avoided the anger of the picket line behind the meshed window of their battle bus as they were transported back and forward through the colliery gates, but their home lives must have been sheer hell. They were given wages and concessionary coal for just sitting around at work, doing nothing, because not one piece of coal was ever mined. Yet on the other side of the picket line, striking miners were left standing in all weathers, seven hours a day, five days a week, for a cup of tea and a meat pie. Little wonder that feelings were running high. The Lynemouth picket line above consisted of: John Simpson, Bill Harris, Bob Monahan and Bob Streener.

Striking miners in the region stood to lose the first £14 of any income. Their working wives lost entitlement to Income Support. Miners who were single received nothing. Any hardship money was paid out of Union funds. Loans were given by Wansbeck Council to families in 'desperate need'. They say an army marches on its stomach, well the same is true of flying pickets. Here we see the four men delegated to kitchen duties for the day: George Scott, Jimmy Collins, Bart Thomas and Pat Gebhard.

The DSSS at Ashington was ill-equipped for such an influx of claims – people were unsure of what they were entitled to. Miners' cars came off the road, many to be sold; mortgages went unpaid; luxuries such as drinking and smoking ceased; only the most basic of food was served up at meal times; marriages broke up; shopkeepers went bust. Finding fuel to keep the home fires burning became a daily chore; wooden fences disappeared overnight; railway embankments were dug up; beaches were cleaned of dross; outcrop coal seams were found and mined.

One miner was buried digging for coals on the cliffside at Newbiggin. He was dead when the rescuers reached him. Photos show Newbiggin man, Brian Priest (top), shifting some rocks, and Russell Marshall also in search of coal under Newbiggin's cliffs only minutes before Fred Taylor, aged forty-seven, of North Seaton Estate, was killed.

This is how the *Newcastle Journal* reported the tragedy on January 22nd 1985:

'Rescuers fought to remove tons of rock trapping a striking miner before the tide overtook them. But although they freed Mr Frederick Taylor, who had been mining an exposed seam on the coast at Newbiggin, he died a few hours later in hospital. Mr James Lillico, another miner, and his schoolteacher son Michael, were walking along the beach when they saw a bicycle near what they realised was a rock fall, and heard Mr Taylor calling for help. But they could see nothing of the trapped man but his hand. While they waited for the emergency services to arrive, they, and some workers from a nearby quarry, used tools from the site to remove smaller rocks. Mr Taylor was completely buried beneath overlapping slabs of sandstone measuring 6ft by 6ft and up to 18 inches thick.

'The inquest heard that when Mr Taylor was uncovered he was in a kneeling position and had been partly driven into the shale by the weight of the stone. Verdict Accidental Death.'

Editor: Yet, surely, father of four, Fred Taylor, was another victim of this bitter drawn-out stoppage.

Bill Harris continues:

Miners' wives were dedicated to their husbands' cause. They showed great determination and energy while attending rallies and marches, and collecting money in support of the strike. They held their own meetings, mostly at Ashington Trade Union Hall, and it was they who decided what course of action should be taken. Some of the Ellington Women's Support Group are seen here: Pat Maughan, Brenda Cunningham, Ann Foggerty, Jacqui Thompson, Karen Kull, Linda Tench, Gwen Newton and Norma Kull.

Gwen Newton who edited some of the women's stories of the stoppage, had this to say: 'We were just ordinary housewives when our men came out on strike. We came from different backgrounds, but with one thing in common: our men were miners and we were proud of them. Nearly everyone in our community has someone who has worked at the pit. There comes a time when you have to say something. Ashington will soon be a ghost town if we do not do something about it. I think a lot of women realised this, and we were behind our men, all the way.'

By the middle of November 1984, 2,282 more miners had returned to work, bringing the total up to 62,000 working miners. But a massive blow to the local miners was when a local NUM Branch Secretary decided to break the Strike and go through the picket line at Ellington Colliery. Shock waves went through the local mining communities. There was disbelief that this could have happened. This heralded the big crack in the striking ranks. Meanwhile, the TUC and Labour Party seemed to sit on the fence with no end of the Strike in sight.

Editor: But by January 1985 the NCB were releasing figures of those local men who had gone back to work. Out of a total workforce of 555 at Ashington Colliery, 162 men were now working. At Ashington Workshops out of a total of 706 there were 331 back at work. And at the Ellington/Lynemouth Combine, from a total 2,323 men, 926 had crossed the picket line and gone back to work.

Finally, on March 3rd 1985, shouts of 'Scabs', 'Scum', 'Traitors', greeted the miners' union leaders' decision to end the Strike, and there were angry scenes outside TUC headquarters. The delegates had voted by 98 to 91 to return to work on Tuesday March 5th 1985. The Miners' Strike was over.

And so it was that the Ellington miners marched through the village of Lynemouth and back to work, heads still held high, with staunch union men, the late Denis Murphy and Sammy Scott in the front line of the parade.

On a secret 'hit list' in 1985, Ashington Colliery, seen here, was given five years to survive. In fact it only lasted three, closing in March 1988. Tot Burns was then the manager. He said: 'The pit was not viable – it had to close. What we have to ensure is that something else is developed on the site. The saddest thing about the closure is the lack of opportunities for employment in Ashington now.'

Many miners carried to the grave their own legacy of working in dusty, cramped, wet and often noisy places down the pit. This was manifested in diseases of the lungs, arthritis, hearing impairment and other mine-related ailments. Above we see Lynemouth's NUM Compensation Secretary, Bill Harris, handing over a cheque for noise-induced hearing loss to Norman Mather in Ashington's Central Club in January 1989. Norman's cheque brought the awards given out to deserving cases to a staggering one million pounds. Compensation paid up to June 1997 was £1,449,376.

The following photos are from happier times on a rainy day, *circa* 1979 when the Miners' Picnic was still enjoying a degree of support and popularity in Bedlington. Here we have former Ellington electrical engineer, later to be an MP, Jack Thompson, in a jovial mood.

Members of Ashington Colliery Band having a breather after performing in the band contest.

Ashington bandsman Ron Cummings enjoys the day in the company of his father.

Miners' leader Arthur Scargill has an unhappy alliance with Labour leader, Michael Foot.

The Ellington Banner and union officials march into the history books, never realising that their colliery would one day stand alone as the last deep-shaft mine in the north of England.

And the Lynemouth Banner was proudly unfurled and displayed during the march down to Attlee Park, the Picnic Field, with no-one dreaming that their own pit closure was imminent.

One of the last Miners' Picnics to be held at Bedlington was in June 1988. As can be seen in this Picnic programme, Ashington Colliery had closed earlier in the year.

The band contest for the Northumberland Miners' Gala is now (year 2000) held on Station Road, Ashington. The bands and banners then proceed to Woodhorn Colliery Museum for the speeches and prize-giving. The once proud Picnic, with its hundreds of spectators and dozens of marching bands, was very much a watered-down affair when this photo was taken in 1998 with only a handful of bands still in existence and even fewer mines and miners. Leading the parade we have Wansbeck MP Denis Murphy with trade union heavyweight Jimmy Napp. Current Northumberland NUM leader, Ian Lavery, is towards the left next to Arthur Scargill.

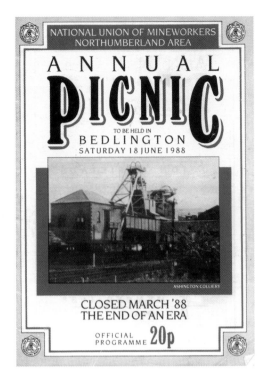

NATIONAL UNION OF MINEWORKERS
NORTHUMBERLAND AREA

ANNUAL

PICNIC

TO BE HELD IN
BEDLINGTON
SATURDAY 18 JUNE 1988

ASHINGTON COLLIERY

CLOSED MARCH '88
THE END OF AN ERA

OFFICIAL
PROGRAMME 20p

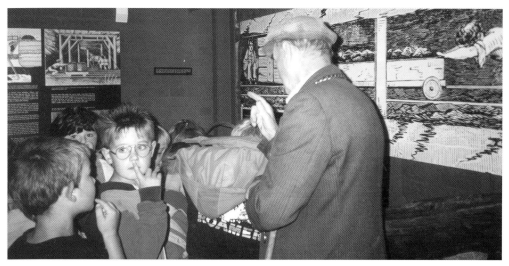

Once Woodhorn Colliery started up as a museum, there was a steady stream of 'old-timers' coming on site who were eager to relive their past by just being close to the winding gear. One of the first regulars was ex-union man and former Scouter, Tommy Davison who, with his pet black labrador, became a permanent fixture, telling visitors his stories from the days when he worked at Woodhorn. Tommy is seen here, around 1993, in a simulated gallery, explaining to a group of children from Windsor First School, Newbiggin, what life was like for a 14-year-old laddie, 'doon the pit'. Little Mark Twizell tells his mate to 'hush up and listen to the way it was'. Others who follow would do well to do the same.

Ellington Colliery struggled on until February 1994 when the new owners, British Coal, decided that enough was enough and, like a modern-day Pontius Pilate, washed its hands of the coal industry in the North altogether. After a year in mothballs, the pit was 'rescued' by RJB Mining, under Mr Richard Budge. Many pundits shook their heads and said that RJB only needed Ellington Pit as a foot-in-the-door – a token gesture to persuade Northumberland County Council that it would be wiser to have open-cast mining on its doorstep, spreading its black cavernous holes and mountains of waste ever wider over the green countryside.

The last pit pony in the whole of Britain was one of four to come out of Ellington Colliery when it had closed for the first time on Friday February 18th 1994. Peter, the 19-year-old pony, came to bank for the last time accompanied by farrier, Keith Adams.

This 1999 Miners' Picnic poster shows some of the magic moments from the past when Coal was King, and life in the mining communities was there to be enjoyed. The memories and the images will linger long after every coalmine in the land has closed.

The People's History

To receive a catalogue of our latest titles send a large SAE to:

The People's History Ltd
Suite 1, Byron House
Seaham Grange Business Park
Seaham, County Durham
SR7 0PY

www.thepeopleshistory.com